D1599271

A Laboratory Manual for Compiler and Operating System Implementation

ELSEVIER COMPUTER SCIENCE LIBRARY

Operating and Programming Systems Series
Peter J. Denning, Editor

Halstead A Laboratory Manual for
Compiler and Operating System Implementation

Programming Languages Series
Thomas E. Cheatham, Editor

Heindel and Roberto Lang-Pak:
An Interactive Language Design System

Theory of Computation Series
Patrick C. Fischer, Editor

Borodin and Munro The Computational
Complexity of Algebraic and Numeric Problems

Computer Design and Architecture Series
Edward J. McCluskey, Editor

Artificial Intelligence Series
Nils J. Nilsson, Editor

A
Laboratory Manual
for
Compiler and
Operating System
Implementation

Maurice H. Halstead

Computer Science Department, Purdue University,

American Elsevier Publishing Company, Inc.

New York   London   Amsterdam

AMERICAN ELSEVIER PUBLISHING COMPANY, INC.
52 Vanderbilt Avenue, New York, N.Y. 10017

ELSEVIER PUBLISHING COMPANY
335 Jan Van Galenstraat, P.O. Box 211
Amsterdam, The Netherlands

International Standard Book Number 0-444-00142-5
Library of Congress Card Number 73-10897

Library of Congress Cataloging in Publication Data

Halstead, Maurice Howard, 1918-
   A laboratory manual for compiler and operating
system implementation.
   (Operating and programming systems series)
   Includes bibliographies.
   1. Compiling (Electronic computers) I. Title.
QA76.6.H32   001.6'425   73-10897
ISBN 0-444-00142-5

Manufactured in the United States of America

To Sylvia

Contents

Preface

During five years of teaching a first course in compiler implementation in the university environment, following a decade of directing software development in industry, it has become clear to the author that there is a need for a learning and teaching aid which is intended to supplement, but not to replace, the growing number of good textbooks in the area.

Just as the classic fields of chemistry and physics were first taught as laboratory sciences, using both textbooks and laboratory manuals, the field of computer software seems well suited to this approach. While an introductory physics text may discuss the results of experiments with cyclotrons or inter-planetary probes, a laboratory manual in physics must be confined to simple exercises which illustrate the basic principles involved. Similarly, the laboratory phase of instruction in the software area should present an opportunity for the student to examine, and preferably to implement, a complete compiler or operating system. Such an objective immediately raises its own group of inter-related problems, however. If the system is too large, then it will not serve the intended purpose. Further, if it is large enough to demonstrate the basic elements, but is written in assembly language, it will still be insufficiently intelligible to serve the purpose, while if it is written in a standard language such as Fortran or Cobol, it cannot demonstrate realistic methods. This part of the problem can be solved by writing the system in a system-oriented language, such as Neliac, Jovial, Bliss, or PL/S; but again, if a compiler for the complete language is shown, the system will be too large. On the other hand, if a *toy* language is designed for this purpose, it will usually be impossible to expand the language without encountering design deficiencies.

A solution to these interrelated problems of size, capability, language level, realism, and extendibility has been obtained by taking the Neliac language, which itself was a real-time systems language derived from Algol, and peeling away some 90 percent. The part which remains is adequate to write a self-compiler, and to write a similarly reduced time-sharing operating system. While the system is intentionally minimal, there can be no danger that its design would be inadequate for expansion into a complete software system, since it was obtained by reducing such a system.

The approach used in this manual, which has enjoyed some measure of success for several hundred students, therefore consists of the presentation of a small, systems-oriented language called Pilot, followed by two completed examples of its use, first to write a compiler, and then to write a time-sharing operating system. In a one-semester course, 85 percent of the students have succeeded in implementing the compiler with from one to fifteen extensions, while covering the bulk of the material in a text such as that of Rosen, Gries, or Donovan.

A list of those texts currently available is given in the references at the end of Chapter 1.

Lafayette, Indiana

Maurice H. Halstead

Prologue

In studying or teaching fundamental concepts involved in both compilers and operating systems, it may be advantageous to have available a compact example of each, to serve as a source of laboratory experiments or semester projects to supplement material covered by the range of available texts in the field.

The first part of this manual provides the material required by a student to enable him to write a specific, minimal self-compiler; to check it out; to extend the source language which it accepts; and to improve the object code which it produces. The second part provides comparable material for the implementation of a skeletal time-slicing operating system. The student will also need, in addition to talent and industry, access to any computer larger than a desk calculator and other than a Univac 1108. The latter restriction arises because the examples of both the compiler and operating system given are instances of implementations for that computer, hence little would be learned by reinstalling them on that particular machine.

The objectives are threefold: (1) to give the student personal familiarity with the more detailed and specific problems which must be solved for any compiler or for any operating system, including that class of problems which appear too trivial to warrant attention in a scientific paper, or even a text, but which nevertheless must be mastered by the implementor himself; (2) to provide a background which will allow more ready assimilation of a text, and of even more advanced papers which will appear in the future; and (3) to provide the student with a frame of reference which should assist him in understanding the multitude of newly discovered or rediscovered techniques in the field of computer software.

Pilot Properties

Although the history of the Pilot language can actually be traced back through the Lockheed Missiles & Space Company to the Navy Electronics Laboratory, one might nevertheless coin the acronym, *P*urdue *I*nstructional

*L*anguage for *O*perating systems and *T*ranslators. Pilot itself has more than a dozen properties which contribute to its usefulness in the present context, each worth a sentence or two by way of explanation.

Efficiency.   Pilot is an inherently efficient language, since virtually all of its features have been designed with both ease of compilation and speed of object code in mind. Many student implementors have produced compilers which would compile the complete compiler from source to target language in 5 seconds on a CDC 6500.

One pass.   Since the Pilot compiler is based upon the one-pass principle, it must therefore illustrate a solution of the *forward reference* problem for those cases in which jumps to as yet uncompiled labels are encountered.

Reentrant.   Both the compiler itself is reentrant (or *pure procedure*), as well as the code which it generates. This feature may be readily omitted, however, if it is not required.

Portable.   The language has been implemented hundreds of times, on most of the large computers and many of the smaller ones, such as the IBM 1130 and IBM 1620.

Systems-orientation.   The language includes notation for reaching core directly, both for fetches and stores, and for transfers. Both octal and hexadecimal numbers are handled. It also allows the insertion of one or more machine-language instructions after any statement. With these capabilities, it is clearly close enough to any machine on which it is implemented to assure the ability to produce efficient code. While it does not otherwise provide for bit handling, such a feature has frequently been added by a student implementor.

Simple language.   The language itself has been reduced to a very basic simplicity, while retaining only those capabilities required to write, for example, a complete compiler. It includes neither floating point, literals, nor parenthetical grouping of expressions, and all variables are global. From the point of view of the user of the language, some of these restrictions may appear irksome, at which point it is well to remember that the user is intended to be the implementor as well, and that the restrictions have been introduced for the sole purpose of easing the task of understanding the implementation. As evidence of this simplicity, one may note that the Backus Normal Form specification of Pilot requires fewer than 30 definitions, of which five are devoted to the differences between octal, decimal, and hexadecimal numbers.

Minimal size.   The Pilot compiler consists of approximately 250 source statements, an order of magnitude fewer than the compiler from which it was reduced. This fact, however, does not imply that the important features of a compiler have been eliminated. One binary order of magnitude was obtained by not including diagnostics, and another by avoiding all but the most trivial form of optimization. While it is true, and must frequently be emphasized, that half of the code in a good compiler should be concerned with error detection, this phase is so highly dependent upon the source language chosen that the amount the student could learn in this area would not warrant the added complexity which it would introduce at this point. While some optimization techniques now have more generality than do diagnostics, they still tend to vary greatly with the architecture of the machine for which they are designed. Since the purpose requires that the compiler be readily implementable upon a wide variety of unspecified computers, the only optimization retained in the compiler is the provision that a single working register not be reloaded when it already contains the desired variable.

Crutch coding. The ability of the compiler to accept a mnemonic or numeric machine-language instruction after any statement is called *crutch coding,* implying the descent to a lower, less intelligible level of language. While this feature is not used in the compiler itself, it is essential in the implementation of the operating system, where efficiency could not be achieved without it. It is worth noting that the crutch-coding generator alone, in the absence of all other generators, provides a simple one-to-one assembler capability.

Hash coding. Since the compiler employs scatter storage addressing, it demonstrates the basic features of the only generally accepted method of handling symbol tables in compilers and assemblers.

CO–NO tables. The Pilot compiler uses a *transition matrix,* called a Current Operator–Next Operator (CO–NO) table for parsing; hence it demonstrates the fastest parsing technique known.

Extensible. Rather than reducing the size of the CO–NO table to correspond to the limited size of Pilot, the matrix has been deliberately left sparse. Any combination of operators preceding and following an operand may be assigned a specific meaning, resulting in a call upon an individual generator. This allows for easy extension, by supplying a new generator for any point in the matrix not previously implemented. Further, because the compiler was obtained by compressing a large working Algol-type compiler, system design problems are avoided when it is expanded.

Modular. Despite the fact that all variables are global, the compiler for Pilot is written in modular fashion. It consists of a driver and 14 subroutines. Consequently, each of these subroutines can be analyzed and understood separately.

Self-compiler. The fact that a source listing of the compiler exists in the same language which it accepts provides several advantages. By compiling the source deck once, and using the output of that compilation to compile the same source deck again, success of the second compilation can be taken as evidence of a "bug-free" compiler. While reaching this moment of truth invariably provides the thrill of accomplishment for the compiler implementor, it also paves the way for the greater thrill, since it makes it possible to make and test extensions quickly. As a result, the student who wishes to design a completely new language facility may do so, and obtain results with a run or two. Further, it illustrates the only known method of avoiding the usual situation, in which it is expected that fast compilation implies slow execution, and, conversely, that producing highly optimized code requires long compilation times. Since any self-compiler must execute only object code which it has itself generated, it must either generate poor code slowly, or excellent code rapidly. In practice, this means that the initial version will usually be slow, but that improvements may constantly be added. This technique has been adopted in the implementation of a number of impressive production compilers, including those for extended Fortran compilers, such as LRLTRAN and Fortran IV-H.

Versatile.   The versatility of the language has been demonstrated in more advanced projects. It has been used by graduate students to write a D level PL/I to Pilot translator in Pilot language. By providing a Pilot compiler for a given computer, they are able to compile their PL/I translator. Then, by feeding the output of their translator to their Pilot compiler, they are able to compile and execute PL/I programs. Other graduate students have used Pilot in thesis research, leading to demonstrations of dynamic algebra, inverse compiling, program simplification, and the reorganization of multipass programs.

PART I. COMPILING SYSTEMS

Chapter 1

Introduction

Since virtually all compilers have much in common, it should be possible to study any good compiler for a language such as Fortran, Algol, Cobol, Jovial or PL/I, and from a detailed analysis of that one compiler on a single machine, to obtain the knowledge which could be readily transferred to or from the others. While possible, such a method is uneconomic in terms of effort, primarily because such compilers, in addition to their fundamental or basic components, must of necessity contain a far larger proportion of code which is concerned only with the details of their particular environment and implementation. With that approach, the trees obscure the forest.

At the other extreme, one could distill, from the population of all compilers, those principles which they exhibit in common, and study them in a completely abstract way. While this extreme holds the advantage over the other, it suffers from a paucity of detail which leaves the student with a compartmentalized knowledge which is often too fragmentary to provide a firm base from which he could design and implement a processor independently. He may recognize a forest, but miss a tree.

Rather than choosing either extreme, this laboratory manual assumes that the broad view may be obtained from an increasing number of good books on compilers and operating systems, but that, in the final analysis, the only way that a student can both know, and know that he knows, this interesting area is to study both the objectives and the details of their implementation. This manual, therefore, provides sufficient detail to enable the student to completely understand and implement both a self-compiler and a time-sharing operating system. While both the self-compiler and the operating system have been obtained by reducing larger systems by an order of magnitude, they still retain the important functions of their predecessors.

Before starting the actual implementation of the compiler illustrated in chapters 1 through 14, it is advisable to consider briefly the various classes of processors which have been developed, and to examine the gross structure of a few of the processes which will be involved.

While there is as yet no satisfactory ordering scheme for programming systems, just as there is no rational method for classifying computer languages by comparison of their level, for the purposes of this manual the following listing should suffice.

Machine coding. The direct preparation of the numerical code of the machine, by writing in the absolute octal, hexadecimal, decimal, or even binary, representation of the computer involved. This is the true machine language.

Simple assemblers. Systems which provide the user with a one-to-one conversion from mnemonic representations of machine operation codes and addresses to machine code. Frequently this is referred to as *machine language.*

Macro assemblers. Systems which augment the capabilities of simple assemblers by allowing the definition of new mnemonic operations not included in the repertoire of instructions of the computer, achieved by a combination of such instructions. This *one-to-many* expansion provides so much more power than that available in a simple assembler that attempts are being made to reduce its customary machine dependence.

Interpreters. Systems which are virtually the same as compilers, except that instead of generating machine code for later execution, they transfer control to a stored routine for actual execution upon recognition of each statement. While interpreters fell into disuse because of their extreme slowness, they are again becoming of interest because of the systems control they provide for multiprogramming real-time systems.

Compilers. Systems which convert higher-level language on a one-to-many basis to machine code, which may be more expeditiously ordered than the original order encountered in the source language.

Cross compilers. Compilers which operate on a given computer, but generate machine code for a different computer.

Compiler-compilers. Systems which provide a mechanism and language for semiautomatic production of compilers.

Self-compilers. A term occasionally used to describe a compiler written in its own language, usually with the proviso that it is intended to be readily extendable in source language and capable of improvement in object-code efficiency.

High-level translators. Systems which translate from a given source language to an object language which in itself is another source language. To date the principle uses of this class of translator has been to translate from one version of a given language to a later version of the same language.

Decompilers. Systems which accept as input the machine language of a given computer, and translate it to a quasi-machine-independent, higher-level language. While to date no decompilers have reduced programmer intervention to zero, they have been economically successful in converting applications programs from one generation of computers to another, and in improving documentation of early machine language programs.

The next dozen chapters concern the implementation of a self-compiler, but as can be seen from preceding definitions, this must also cover a compiler. In addition, by virtue of the inclusion of a machine language statement type in the language definition, the self-compiler will be seen to include a simple assembler.

To prepare for these exercises, we will start by considering the broad outlines of two processes, the structure of a compiler, and the process of transferring a self-compiler from one computer to another.

The basic elements of a compiler must provide for:

1. Accepting source language from an input device
2. Converting from the binary-coded-decimal (BCD) or similar input code of the device to a more efficient internal compiler code (ICC)
3. Scanning the source string to determine which actions are required
4. Generating the proper code, either in an intermediate or machine language form.

Beyond these basic functions, a compiler should also provide facilities for:

1. Diagnosing errors
2. Deleting redundant expressions
3. Allocating working registers
4. Optimizing and relocating object code
5. Providing various compile-time statistics

Since these additional features are left as options to the student, and only the basic functions are demonstrated in the compiler, we may accept Fig. 1.1 as an illustration of the compiling process.

From Fig. 1.1, it can be noted that some combinations found in the source string, in ICC, will result in the immediate generation of object code, while others, such as labels, will merely result in the saving of information for later use by the compiler.

Transferring a Self-compiler

Suppose one has implemented a compiler for some language L, written in the machine or assembly language of computer X, and producing object code for computer X, and assume that a compiler for the same language is needed on, and for, a new computer Y. In this case, except for the personal experience gained, there is nothing in the original X compiler that will be of much help in producing the new Y compiler. However, if the original X compiler had also been a self-compiler, then the situation would have been somewhat different, because there would have been a source listing (and card deck) of the original X

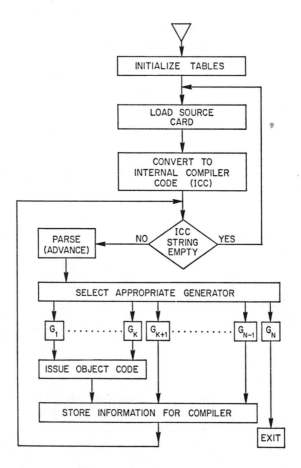

Fig. 1.1. The compiling process.

compiler in language L. Since there is to be no change in language L, none of those parts of the compiler which deal solely with the properties of language L will require any change. The only changes required in the source listing will be in: (1) the object code issued by the generators, and (2) any of the routines which depend upon the word length or character code of the machine. Let us call item 2 the *housekeeping* function, and leave it without change for the moment. If we prepare a new source deck, identical to the original, except for the generators, which we revise to make them issue the object code appropriate to the new computer Y, then we will have a source deck which can still be compiled by the original compiler. When this compilation has been performed, the result will be a new compiler, or strictly speaking, a *cross-compiler*. This cross-compiler will still run only on the original machine, X, but it will produce

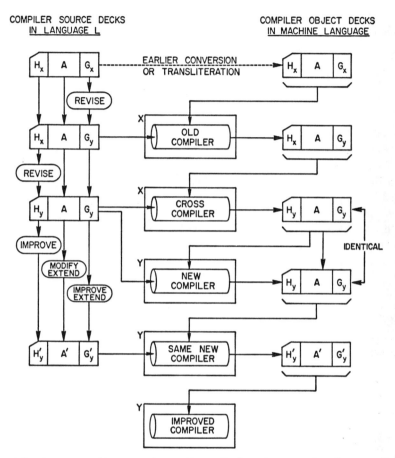

COMPILER SOURCE DECKS
IN LANGUAGE L

COMPILER OBJECT DECKS
IN MACHINE LANGUAGE

| H_x | A | G_x |

EARLIER CONVERSION
OR TRANSLITERATION

| H_x | A | G_x |

REVISE

| H_x | A | G_y |

X OLD COMPILER

| H_x | A | G_y |

REVISE

| H_y | A | G_y |

X CROSS COMPILER

| H_y | A | G_y |

IMPROVE

MODIFY EXTEND

IMPROVE EXTEND

Y NEW COMPILER

| H_y | A | G_y |

IDENTICAL

| H'_y | A' | G'_y |

Y SAME NEW COMPILER

| H'_y | A' | G'_y |

Y IMPROVED COMPILER

Fig. 1.2. The process of bootstrapping a self-compiler from Computer X to Computer Y.

object code which will only run on the new machine, Y. At first glance it might appear that the source listing (with its revised generators) which produced the cross-compiler could be compiled by the cross-compiler to produce a compiler which would run on, and for, the new machine. While this is almost true, in practice it is necessary to revise the housekeeping routines in the source listing before doing so.

The process is shown in Fig. 1.2, in which the symbology has the following meaning. The column on the left contains source decks of the various versions of the compilers, always written in the same language, L. Each deck contains a complete compiler, and consists of the three parts: housekeeping, H; analysis, A: and generators, G. The subscripts denote the machine for which the component has been specialized. Since the analysis portion is machine independent, it is not subscripted. The source language compiler decks in the left-hand column must be changed, by hand, to produce the next version below them, and must be submitted to a compiler running in a computer in the middle column in order to produce the machine language deck in the right-hand column. The middle column contains the computers X and Y, denoted by the **rectangles**. Each of the rectangles contains a compiler, denoted by the **cylinders**, in its own machine language, which has been obtained by installing the appropriate deck from the right-hand column. The **broken arrow** represents a conversion made on a still-earlier computer, or even a manual transliteration if the earlier version is unavailable.

Studying the process shown in Fig. 1.2, it is apparent that as soon as the generators have been revised, the cross-compiler can be produced. At this point, any program written in language L can be executed on machine Y, by compiling on machine X and carrying the object deck to the new machine. Cases do arise in practice in which this is the final step, when for example, computer Y is too small to contain its own compiler. The term *bootstrapping*, used in Fig. 1.2, has been used by different authors to denote either the first part of the process, transferring to a new computer, or, more frequently, the second part of the process, that of extending and expanding a compiler on a given computer, in this case machine Y.

Bootstrapping Pilot

This manual contains a source listing in language L, where L denotes Pilot; for machine X; where X denotes Univac 1108, but assumes that only machine Y is available to the student. With this assumption, the process reduces to that shown in Fig. 1.3.

The box labeled *transliterate* represents a manual process, which can be accomplished in any of a number of ways, once the revised listing, in Pilot, has been completed. If the available computer already has a good macro assembler, it will be best to use it, by rewriting the revised listing in the macro-assembly language of machine Y, and assembling to produce Version O. Note that the usual need for efficiency in compilers does not apply to Version O, since it will be used only once. If a macro assembler is not available on machine Y, the second choice would be a high-level language such as Fortran or Cobol, or even better, Algol or PL/I. SNOBOL has also been used, but with that language, machine time requirements tend to be extremely great. In the absence of any of these, the most time-consuming process must be resorted to, that of rewriting in straight assembly language.

It is interesting to consider the fact that, in principle, this transliteration

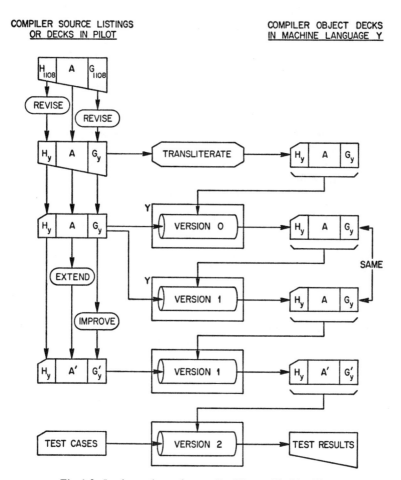

COMPILER SOURCE LISTINGS
OR DECKS IN PILOT

COMPILER OBJECT DECKS
IN MACHINE LANGUAGE Y

Fig. 1.3. Implementing and extending Pilot on Machine Y.

process could be performed in an entirely different way. It is possible to produce the machine code Version O by desk-checking a copy of the revised source listing through itself. While this approach is possible, the amount learned would not be commensurate with the labor expended. Even so, this latter approach is the only one which would guarantee that Version 0 and Version 1 would be identical. With the recommended methods, differences are bound to occur, but these should be avoided whenever possible, so that when program bugs are detected and removed from Version 0, they can simultaneously be removed from the deck which produces Version 1.

General References or Course Texts

Coffman, Jr., E. G. and Denning, P. J. *Operating Systems Theory*. Englewood Cliffs, N.J.: Prentice-Hall, 1973.

Cuttle, G. and Robinson, D. B. (eds.). *Executive Programs and Operating Systems*. New York: American Elsevier, 1970.

Donovan, John J. *Systems Programming*. New York: McGraw-Hill, 1972.

Ершова, А. П. ред. «*АЛЬФА, система автоматизации программирования*», Новосибирск, 1967.

Gauthier, Richard and Ponto, Stephen, *Designing Systems Programs*. New York: Prentice-Hall, 1970.

Grau, A. A., Hill, U. and Langmaack, H. *Translation of Algol 60*. Berlin: Springer, 1967.

Gries, David *Compiler Construction for Digital Computers*. New York: Wiley, 1971.

Hopgood, F. R. A. *Compiling Techniques*. New York: American Elsevier, 1969.

Katzen, Jr., H. *Operating Systems: A Pragmatic Approach*. New York: Van Nostrand Reinhold, 1973.

McKeeman, William M., Horning, James J., and Wortman, David *A Compiler Generator*. Englewood Cliffs, N.J.: Prentice-Hall, 1970.

Pollack, Bary W. (ed). *Compiler Techniques*. Philadelphia: Auerbach, 1972.

Rosen, Saul (ed.) *Programming Systems and Languages*. New York: McGraw-Hill, 1967.

Watson, R. W. *Time Sharing System Design Concepts*. New York: McGraw-Hill, 1970.

Wilkes, M. V., "Time Sharing Computer Systems," 2 ed. New York, American Elsevier, 1972.

Chapter 2

Structural Design of the Pilot Compiler

The Pilot self-compiler consists of the 14 subroutines:

A. NEXT CARD
B. READ NUMBER
C. READ NAME
D. NAME DEFINITION
E. ADVANCE
F. BUILD COMMAND
G. COMP DECLARATIONS
H. SAVE FORWARD REFERENCES
I. FILL FORWARD REFERENCES
J. COMP VERB LIST
K. BUILD SUBROUTINE
L. END SUBROUTINE
M. COMPILE PILOT
N. INITIALIZE LISTS

These are preceded by a single noun list containing all of the tables and variables which the subroutines require. They will be presented in Chapters 4 through 13 as they would operate on, and produce code for, a Univac 1108. The actual programs for each of these subroutines will appear as Verb Lists A through N, and the combined declaration statement will be divided and presented by parts in Noun Lists A through N.

While the subroutines ADVANCE, COMP DECLARATIONS, and COMP VERB LIST constitute the heart of the compiler, each of the other subroutines is required, and since they illustrate general features employed in virtually all compilers, they will all be presented in complete detail. Rather than introducing them in their order of importance, or even of complexity, however, they will be discussed in the order in which they might well be written and tested.

In the actual design of a compiler, as in the design of any program, it is clear that the driver, or the routine which calls upon the submodules, should be held

9

in mind from the onset. On the other hand, the program, once designed, should
be implemented from the bottom up, for only in that way can it be built from
tested components. Consequently the driver, in this case COMPILE PILOT, will
be detailed almost last (see Chapter 12).

Little attempt will be made to distinguish between machine-dependent and
machine-independent processes; hence a thorough understanding of each subroutine and its interrelations with the others will be required in order to convert
to an available computer. To ease this task somewhat, a subroutine map of the
compiler is given in Fig. 2.1. This map is distinctly different from a flow chart,
but in this case it is much more useful. Since each of the 14 modules of the

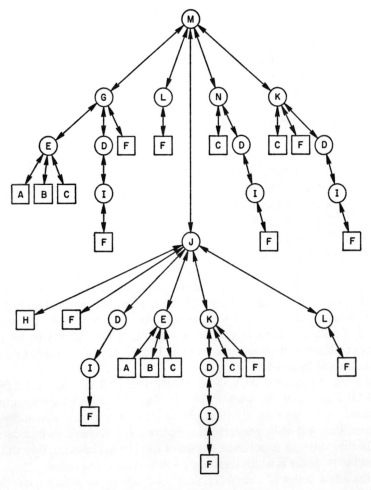

Fig. 2.1. Pilot subroutine map.

compiler is written as a closed subroutine (with global parameters), it must return to the subroutine which called it that time. By using a technique called *node-splitting*, which simply means that we will make copies of any blocks which occur in overlapping loops, we can represent all possible paths among the 14 subroutines. In the subroutine map, any path which is entered must be traversed twice, first downward and later upward. Rectangular blocks are used to represent subroutines which are *grounded*, or do not themselves ever call other subroutines. It is interesting to note that, to form the map of 14 subroutines, a total of 41 copies are required. From this one can infer that the modular design has eliminated a considerable amount of effort.

References

Glass, Robert L. An elementary discussion of compiler/interpreter writing. *Computing Surveys,* 1:15, 1969.

Mendocino, S. F., Hughes, R. A., Martin, J. T., McMahon, F. H., Ranelletti, J. E., and Zwakenberg, R. G. The LRLTran compiler. *Comm. Assoc. Computing Machinery* 3:366, 1965.

Chapter 3

The BNF Definition of a Language

The following 29 productions or definitions constitute a complete syntax of the basic Pilot language. These definitions are written in a slightly simplified form of BNF (Backus-Naur form) notation, in which single letters and single graphics represent themselves as terminal symbols, while occurrences of two letters together represent individual members of the class identified by those two letters.

The special symbol ::= may be translated either as "consists of" or as "is defined to be." The special symbol | may be translated as "or of," and a blank or space between symbols represents "followed by." Note that, for example, the expression A|B C|D yields the set $\{A, BC, D\}$ rather than the set $\{AC, AD, BC, BD\}$. In Table 3.1, the descriptive words on the left are not a part of the actual definition.

Not included in Table 3.1 are the facts that a double slash, / /, indicates that a comment follows and completes the line or card, and that names must be unique in their first n characters, where n may be selected to fit a given computer.

Now let us examine Table 3.1 in some detail, to see what we can, and what we cannot, learn about a language from its BNF definition.

Let us start with the definition of a jump:

$$JU ::= OP .$$

which may be interpreted as: A member of the class JU consists of a member of the class OP followed by a period. We must now look for a definition of OP, and find:

$$OP ::= NA|NA\ SS|SS$$

which gives us the information that an operand can consist of a name, or of a subscripted name, or of a subscript alone.

Do the definitions provide any way to determine whether any name used as an operand must also have been used as a label? If not, would it be legal to jump to a particular entry in a noun list? Considering the second alternative, a jump to a subscripted name, does this imply the existence of a crude switch, or "calcu-

TABLE 3.1.

Pseudo-BNF Syntax of the Pilot Language

Routine	RT ::= NL ; ; LA VL . .
Noun list	NL ::= DC|NL , DC
Declaration	DC ::= NA|NA = NR|FA|NA [NR] |NA : NR
Filled array	FA ::= NA [NR] = NR|FA , NR
Verb list	VL ::= ST|VL ST
Statement	ST ::= AS|CO|SR|JU|CA|RD|WR|CR|LA ST
Assignment	AS ::= OP → OP ,| OP AR OP → OP
Comparison	CO ::= OP RE OP : JU ;
Subroutine	SR ::= LA { VL }
Jump	JU ::= OP .
Call	CA ::= OP ,
Read	RD ::= > NA < ,
Write	WR ::= < NA > ,
Crutch	CR ::= $ NR , NR ;|$ NR , NA ;|$ NA , NR ;|$ NA , NA ;
Arithmetic	AR ::= +|−|*|/
Relational	RE ::= =|<
Operand	OP ::= NA|NA SS|SS
Subscript	SS ::= [IN]
Label	LA ::= NA :
Name	NA ::= LE|NA LE|NA NR
Number	NR ::= 0 0 HN| 0 ON|DN|0
Letter	LE ::= A|B|C|D|E|F|G|H|I|N|O|P|Q|R|S|T|U|V|W|X|Y|Z
Index	IN ::= I|J|K|L|M|N
Hexanumber	HN ::= HD|HN HD|HN 0
Decimalnr	DN ::= DD|DN DD|DN 0
Octalnr	ON ::= OD|ON OD|ON 0
Octaldig	OD ::= 1|2|3|4|5|6|7
Decimaldig	DD ::= 8|9|OD
Hexidig	HD ::= A|B|C|D|E|F|DD

lated go to" in the language? The third alternative, a jump to a member of the class *SS*, which might be written:

[J] .

is rather different, since its meaning is not apparent either from the BNF definitions directly, nor from even a thorough familiarity with any general-purpose language. As we shall see later when compiling them, operands which consist of bracketed letters alone refer to actual machine locations; thus, in the example above, had the value of *J* been 2000 at the time the jump was executed, control would have passed to location 2000 in core. While this feature would be dangerous in a general-purpose language, it can be used to advantage by the systems implementor.

Turning to the definition of a *filled array*, is it obvious that a table of fixed size with initial values could be entered in a noun list as, for example:

$$SQUARES \ [7] = 0,1,4,9,16,25,36,$$

On the other hand, is there any way in which the BNF definition could provide the information that the Pilot compiler will subscript all arrays by starting with zero, rather than with one, so that in the above case, the assignments

$$05 \rightarrow J,$$
$$SQUARES[J] \rightarrow ANSWER,$$

will actually leave the value 25 (not 16) in the word ANSWER? Similarly, there is no way to tell from the BNF definitions whether the compiler will test for index values exceeding the range of an array at execution time. Since the basic Pilot compiler does not, we will take advantage of this disadvantage, by judiciously ordering arrays and biasing indices, as we shall see in the subroutine INITIALIZE in Verb List N (p. 72.)

Next, examine the definitions of number, decimal number, octal number and hexadecimal number. Is it apparent that leading zeros have been given an unusual function, so that, for example, the decimal number 26 could be represented as:

$$26 = 032 = 001A$$

Now, tracing through lower and lower definition levels from the definition of a verb list, determine whether basic Pilot allows any numeric literals in the procedure portion of a routine. Does your result suggest an extension which you might make to the basic compiler as soon as you have it running? In the meantime, how might you proceed? In a noun list, the declarations:

$$ZERO = 0,$$
$$ONE = 1,$$

are obviously legal, but rather cumbersome. Test the definition of name, noting its recursive nature. Provided a name starts with a letter, can the following characters constitute a decimal number? Then, provided one can remember to keypunch the letter *O* instead of the digit *0* as a first character, might not the noun list entries:

$$O = 0,$$
$$O1 = 1,$$
$$O2 = 2,$$

offer a less cumbersome alternative?

Turn next to the definition of assignment statements, and note the lack of recursion there. This implies, correctly, that the interesting area of compiling algebraic expressions will be treated as an extension, rather than an inherent feature of the basic compiler.

Continuing to study the BNF definitions, one can still learn more by noting things that are not present. For example, there are no key words or reserved words in the language. Neither is there a block structure. Since each program must consist of only one set of declaration statements, or noun list, and one set of executable statements, or verb list, all operands must actually be global. This will require that if an operand is to be used as a local variable within a given module, it must have a unique name.

References

Backus, J. W. "The Syntax and Semantics of the Proposed International Algorithmic Language of the Zurich ACM-GAMM Conference." *Proceedings of an International Conference on Information Processing,* Paris: UNESCO, 1959, pp. 125–132.

Nauer, P. (ed.). Revised report on the algorithmic language Algol 60. 6: 1, 1963.

Chapter 4

Defining an Internal Compiler Code

The BCD, Fieldata, EBCDIC (*E*xtended *B*inary *C*oded *D*ecimal *I*nterchange *C*ode), ASCII (*A*merican *S*tandards *C*ode for *I*nformation *I*nterchange), or other codes available for various input devices are neither completely standard nor well suited to the specialized logical requirements of the compilation process. Since they must be concerned with data-transmission problems, collating sequences, and hardware developments, this situation may change rather slowly. As a consequence, in order to obtain greater efficiency and a slight measure of machine independence, conversion to an *internal compiler code* (ICC) is usually required.

While there are one or two obvious design criteria for such a code, and others which are slightly more subtle, virtually no work on truly optimum ordering has been done.

Basically, each operator, each digit, and each letter which is legal in the language must have a unique numerical value, or bit pattern, assigned to it. In addition, it should be possible to distinguish between an operator and the first character of an operand with a single comparison. Consequently, the code must be so ordered that the numerical equivalents of operators must either be all greater or all less than the values for letters and numbers.

Similarly, one numerical comparison should suffice to differentiate between a digit and a letter. Does it matter which comes first? Consider the case of hexadecimal digits. As we will see in the subroutine READ NUMBER, a real increase in efficiency results if the numeric value of the A is one greater than the code value of the 9. This suggests that a suitable code might be obtained by starting with the 10 decimal digits, zero through 9, following them with the 26 letters, A through Z, and then following them with as many operators as a given language requires. This arrangement would yield the desired advantage in the subroutine READ NUMBER, but it would slow the process of analyzing operators; hence it is customary to start with the operators, followed by the digits, and completed by the letters.

The basic Pilot language uses only 17 different operators, but in order to permit extensions to the language, several more have been included in the ICC. The pattern used in the following exercises is given in Table 4.1.

TABLE 4.1.
Internal Compiler Code (ICC)

Name	Character	Decimal	Octal	Hexadecimal
Period	.	0	00	000
Comma	,	1	01	001
Colon	:	2	02	002
Replace	→	3	03	003
Plus	+	4	04	004
Minus	−	5	05	005
Multiply	*	6	06	006
Divide-Slash	/	7	07	007
Equal	=	8	010	008
Less than	<	9	011	009
Crutch	$	10	012	00A
Left bracket	[	11	013	00B
Begin SR	{ or ↓	12	014	00C
End SR	} or ↑	13	015	00D
Semicolon	;	14	016	00E
Greater than	>	15	017	00F
Right bracket	]	16	020	0010
Left paren	(	17	021	0011
Right paren	)	18	022	0012
And	∧	19	023	0013
Or	∨	20	024	0014
Not	¬	21	025	0015
Not equal	≠	22	026	0016
Less or equal	≤	23	027	0017
Greater or equal	≥	24	030	0018
Prime	' or ≡	25	031	0019
Unused		26	032	001A
Zero	0	27	033	001B
One	1	28	034	001C
Two	2	29	035	001D
Three	3	30	036	001E
Four	4	31	037	001F
Five	5	32	040	0020
Six	6	33	041	0021
Seven	7	34	042	0022
Eight	8	35	043	0023
Nine	9	36	044	0024
	A	37	045	0025
	B	38	046	0026
	C	39	047	0027
	D	40	050	0028
	E	41	051	0029
	F	42	052	002A
	G	43	053	002B
	H	44	054	002C
	I	45	055	002D
	J	46	056	002E
	K	47	057	002F

Table 4.1. (Continued)

Name	Character	Decimal	Octal	Hexadecimal
	L	48	060	0030
	M	49	061	0031
	N	50	062	0032
	O	51	063	0033
	P	52	064	0034
	Q	53	065	0035
	R	54	066	0036
	S	55	067	0037
	T	56	070	0038
	U	57	071	0039
	V	58	072	003A
	W	59	073	003B
	X	60	074	003C
	Y	61	075	003D
	Z	62	076	003E
Blank	ƀ	63	077	003F

Having devised an ICC, it is only necessary to obtain a copy of the BCD or equivalent input code available for one's own machine in order to set up the conversion table which will be required in using a *table look-up* when executing the subroutine NEXT CARD. Using the following list declaration as a guide, prepare and keypunch a table suitable for your target machine. The objective is simply to order it in such a way that when the numerical equivalent of a character delivered by an input device is used as an index to the table, the proper ICC value will be reached.

In the example, a 64-character Fieldata code having all of the characters desired is being used. In Fieldata, however, the letters A through Z occupy positions 6 through 31, the digits 0 through 9 occupy positions 48 through 57, and the other symbols are distributed among the intervening positions.

ICC TABLE [64] =

//	Λ	[	]	¬	→	ƀ	A	B
	19,	11,	16,	21,	3,	63,	37,	38,
//	C	D	E	F	G	H	I	J
	39,	40,	41,	42,	43,	44,	45,	46,
//	K	L	M	N	O	P	Q	R
	47,	48,	49,	50,	51,	52,	53,	54,
//	S	T	U	V	W	X	Y	Z
	55,	56,	57,	58,	59,	60,	61,	62,
//	)	–	+	<	=	>	V	$
	18,	5,	4,	9,	8,	15,	20,	10,
//	*	(	{	:	≥	≤	,	}
	6,	17,	12,	2,	24,	23,	1,	13,
//	0	1	2	3	4	5	6	7
	27,	28,	29,	30,	31,	32,	33,	34,
//	8	9	'	;	/	.		≠
	35,	36,	25,	14,	7,	0,	26,	22,

The example above is adequate for the simple case, but frequently there are an inadequate number of characters on the input device (on the 026 keypunch, for example), or even with a full octal hundred characters, those available are not identical with those required. In the latter case, one merely chooses the most nearly reasonable substitutions possible.

For the case of a limited input character set, more serious considerations apply. If the listing device has a full 64-character set, as most do, then one is tempted to merely overpunch the missing characters. If not, the best route open is to select one symbol as an escape character, double the length of the table, and enter the missing characters in the new portion. Then, whenever the escape character is encountered, the character immediately following it is translated from the new half by adding 64 to its BCD value. For example, using the prime as an escape character, the missing characters might be represented as in Table 4.2.

TABLE 4.2.
ICC Character Substitution

Missing character	Substitution	Missing character	Substitution
;	',	>	'G
:	'.	<	'L
[	'(	≥	'2
]	')	≤	'5
→	'=	∧	'A
{	'B (Begin)	∨	'O
}	'E (End)		

While such a substitution will actually slow the compiler, it is unavoidable in some cases, and is probably preferable to double punching in case one is not doing his own keypunching.

Chapter 5

The Lexical Scan

The basic purpose of the *lexical scan,* embodied in the subroutine NEXT CARD, is:

1. To read a card into the array BUFFER
2. To unpack it
3. To translate to internal compiler code (ICC)
4. To remove both spaces and remarks
5. To store the translated characters, one per word, in the array SOURCE
6. To return the count of characters in LAST CHAR POINTER, and reset the global pointer I to the first character.

This subroutine is written in a slightly machine-independent form which could readily be improved for any particular computer. It is designed to illustrate a method for handling unpacking of characters on ones-complement machines, without requiring shifting or masking. When the compiler has been extended to include shifting or logical operations, they would be employed to immediate advantage here.

NEXT CARD, as given in Verb List A, is called only from the subroutine ADVANCE, or Verb List E, and does not itself call any subroutines. Verb List A makes use of 22 operands, divided among the classes shown in Operand Table A.

The global variable I is used throughout the compiler as a pointer to the next character to be scanned in the source string, and will be used for no other purpose. In the same way, when the global variable J is encountered later, it will always be used to point to the next word of object code being generated.

Operand Table A, like those included in later chapters, is not a part of the compiler itself. Instead, it is provided as an aid to the implementor, so that the use of global constants and variables can be quickly identified. Of even more value is the information which shows which global variables are *busy-on-entry* to this subroutine, indicating that there is a path through the subroutine along which the value of the variable will be fetched before it is calculated within the subroutine.

20

Operand Table A

Operand	Class	Used in verb list:	Busy-on-entry	Busy-on-exit
O	Global constant	A,B,C,E,F,G,H,I,J,N.	—	—
O1	Global constant	A,B,C,E,F,G,H,I,J,K,N.	—	—
I	Global pointer	A,B,C,E,J,K,N	No	Yes
K	Local pointer	A,G,I,N	No	No
L	Local pointer	A,H,N	No	No
M	Local pointer	A,J	No	No
BCD BLANKS	Local constant	A	—	—
BCD CHAR	Local variable	A	No	No
BCD SLASH	Local constant	A	—	—
BLANK BCD	Local constant	A	—	—
BUFFER	Local variable	A	No	No
CHAR MASK	Local constant	A	—	—
CHAR PER WORD	Local constant	A	—	—
ICC TABLE	Local constant	A	—	—
LAST CHAR PTR	Global variable	A,E,N	No	Yes
MASK	Local variable	A	No	No
NEG FLAG	Local variable	A	No	No
REMARK FLAG	Local variable	A	No	No
SHIFT	Local constant	A	—	—
SOURCE	Global variable	A,B,C,E,J,K	No	Yes
WORD MASK	Local constant	A	—	—
WORDS PER CARD	Local constant	A	—	—

Similarly, a global variable which is *busy-on-exit* from the subroutine contains a value which will be used by the calling subroutine (or perhaps by a subroutine which calls the calling subroutine).

That part of the complete noun list which is referenced by this subroutine is presented first, and there are several points to be noted. First, while fairly long names are used for nouns and labels, they are all unique within their first six characters. Second, the initial values for all local constants in this noun list are completely dependent upon the machine. Third, the operands *I* through *N* are not listed, since their presence is implied.

Noun List A

BCD BLANKS [6] = 050505050505, 0505050505, 05050505, 050505,
                 0505, 05,
BCD CHAR,
BCD SLASH = 61,

```
BLANK BCD = 05,
BUFFER[14],
CHAR MASK = 077,
CHARS PER WORD = 6,

ICC TABLE[0100] = 19, 11, 16, 21,  3, 63, 37, 38,
                  39, 40, 41, 42, 43, 44, 45, 46,
                  47, 48, 49, 50, 51, 52, 53, 54,
                  55, 56, 57, 58, 59, 60, 61, 62,
                  18,  5,  4,  9,  8, 15, 20, 10,
                   6, 17, 12,  2, 24, 23,  1, 13,
                  27, 28, 29, 30, 31, 32, 33, 34,
                  35, 36, 25, 14,  7,  0, 26, 22,

LAST CHAR POINTER,
MASK,
NEG FLAG,
O = 0,
O1 = 1,
REMARK FLAG,
SHIFT[6] = 010000000000, 0100000000, 01000000, 010000, 0100, 01,
SOURCE[80],
WORD MASK = 07777777777,
WORDS PER CARD = 14;;
```

The use of the two six-word arrays BCD BLANKS and SHIFT will become apparent in the following subroutine, if one remembers that the target machine has a 36-bit word structure, and that the Fieldata code for a blank is a 5.

The subroutine NEXT CARD is bound to be the most machine-dependent part of the compiler, no matter what computer it is implemented on. The problems to be solved can be listed as:

1. To read a unit of a program to be compiled into memory. In the case under discussion, the unit is one 80-column card, and memory consists of 36-bit words. By allowing six bits for each of the 80 characters, we can see that since $(80 \times 6) \div 36 = 13.3$, we will need a 14-word array to hold the characters, still in binary coded decimal (BCD), or in Fieldata code, being read.

2. To unpack characters. This process can be done on any machine having an integer divide by a simple, though inefficient trick. To obtain the first, or leftmost, character, divide the word by a number which will leave the desired character as the quotient, and the lower-ordered characters as remainder. To obtain the second character, first multiply that quotient by the original divisor, and subtract from the original word. The second character can then be obtained from the remaining characters by dividing by a second divisor. The process can be repeated until all of the characters have been unpacked. As an example, assume that the six characters of START:, in their external representation, are to be unpacked from a 36-bit word. Working backward from the ICC table in Chapter 4 (p. 18), we note that the word would contain, in octal notation, the value: 303106273153. Dividing by 10000000000 octal gives a quotient of 30 octal, or 030. Using this value as an index to the table, we find that ICC TABLE[030] = 55, the proper ICC for an *S*. Now if we multiply 030 by 010000000000 and subtract, we have:

$$303106273153$$
$$-300000000000$$
$$\overline{}$$
$$3106273153.$$

Dividing now by 0100000000, we obtain 031 as the second character, and ICC TABLE[031] = 56, corresponding to a *T*. Repeating the process:

$$3106273153$$
$$-3100000000$$
$$\overline{}$$
$$6273153.$$

Dividing now by 01000000, ICC TABLE[06] = 37, corresponding to an *A*. Repeating,

$$6273153$$
$$-6000000$$
$$\overline{}$$
$$273153.$$

Dividing now by 010000, ICC TABLE[027] = 54, or *R*. Again:

$$273153$$
$$-270000$$
$$\overline{}$$
$$3153$$

which gives ICC TABLE[03] = 56, or *T* when divided by 0100. Finally,

$$3153$$
$$-3100$$
$$\overline{}$$
$$53$$

yields ICC TABLE [053] = 2, or : .

   3. To handle negative values resulting from the packing of characters. The technique illustrated above operates smoothly only half the time. The exception occurs when the external code for the leftmost character is greater than 011111 binary, 37 octal, or 31 decimal. When this case occurs, the highest-order bit is obviously a 1, but because this bit is the sign bit on many machines, the arithmetic processes outlined above encounter an apparently negative word. Appropriate countermeasures must be employed to solve this problem. While the solution is not difficult, it is not intuitively obvious, and best illustrated by an example. Suppose that the packed characters considered earlier had consisted instead of the string :START. We then would have found the octal value: 533031062731, but since the leading 5 would set the sign bit to negative, the value would be treated as such. If we first subtract it from zero, we get: 244746715046. Now when we divide by 010000000000 we obtain 024 as the first character, and 4746715046 as the remaining five characters. For the first character:

$$
\begin{array}{r}
077 \\
-024 \\
\hline
053
\end{array}
$$

and for the remaining characters:

$$
\begin{array}{r}
07777777777 \\
-04746715046 \\
\hline
03031062731
\end{array}
$$

which corrects the error and returns the process to the previous condition, since only the first character can cause the problem.

4. *To eliminate blanks.* Since Knuth has shown that in large samples of Fortran programs, about half the columns were blank, it would not do to remove them one at a time.

5. *To eliminate comments.* This requires that when a single slash is encountered, it be converted to the proper ICC value for a divide sign, but when two consecutive slashes are encountered, both of them must be eliminated, together with the remaining characters on the card.

In Verb List A, the algorithms used to implement these solutions is shown. Note that if the external representation for a blank had been greater than 037, as on some machines it is, then the algorithm would have required modification.

Verb List A

```
NEXT CARD: {
    > BUFFER <      / / Read a card into the array buffer.
    < BUFFER >      / / Print immediately as an aid in debugging.
    0 → REMARK FLAG,
    0 → NEG FLAG,
```

```
O → I,
O → K,

NEXT WORD:
    O → L,  / / L will point to the character being extracted.
    BUFFER[K] < O:  SET NEGATIVE.;

TEST BLANKS: / / This will find trailing blanks, but not embedded blanks.
    BUFFER[K] = BCD BLANKS[L]: SKIP BLANKS.;
        BUFFER[K] /SHIFT[L] → BCD CHAR,
        BCD CHAR * SHIFT[L] → MASK,
        BUFFER[K] - MASK → BUFFER[K],
        NEG FLAG = O:  TEST CHAR.;
            WORD MASK - BUFFER[K] → BUFFER[K],
            CHAR MASK - BCD CHAR → BCD CHAR,
            O → NEG FLAG,

TEST CHAR:
    BCD CHAR = BLANK BCD:  NEXT CHAR.;
        BCD CHAR = BCD SLASH:  TEST REMARK.;
            O → REMARK FLAG,

CONVERT:
    BCD CHAR → M,
    ICC TABLE[M] → SOURCE[I],
    I + O1 → I,

NEXT CHAR:
    L + O1 → L,
    L < CHARS PER WORD:  TEST BLANKS.;

SKIP BLANKS:
    K + O1 → K,
    K < WORDS PER CARD:  NEXT WORD.;
        EXIT NC.

TEST REMARK:
    REMARK FLAG = O1:  CLEAR REMARK.;
        O1 → REMARK FLAG,
        CONVERT.

SET NEGATIVE:
    O - BUFFER[K] → BUFFER[K],
    O1 → NEG FLAG,
    TEST BLANKS.

CLEAR REMARK: / / Eliminate the erroneously entered divide sign.
    1 - O1 → 1,

EXIT NC:
    1 → LAST CHAR POINTER,
    O → 1, }
```

After studying the algorithm given in the 36 statements above, one should consider the requirements of his own target machine and devise a comparable algorithm. Then, after that version has been written in the source language, it should be rewritten in either the assembly language or any higher-level language available on the target machine and then tested.

References

Johnson, W., Porter, J., Ackley, S., and Ross, D. Automatic generation of efficient lexical processors using finite state techniques. *Comm. Assoc. Computing Machinery* 11:805, 1968.
Knuth, D. E. An empirical study of Fortran programs. *Software–Practice and Experience* 1:105, 1971.
Lowry, E. S. and Medlock, C. W. Object code optimization. *Comm. Assoc. Computing Machinery* 12:13, 1969.

Chapter 6

Number Conversion

By noting an example, one can see the basic problems involved in reading fixed-point numbers, be they in octal, decimal, or hexadecimal notation, and converting them to the base used by any target machine.

First, consider the number 13. As punched on a card it will be represented by two binary coded decimal (BCD) characters, say, a 49 followed by a 51. This will be unpacked and converted to internal compiler code (ICC) by NEXT CARD, leaving the value 28 in word I of SOURCE, and a 30 in word $I + 1$. Since the scan is forward, the representation of the first digit, 28, will be encountered first. Notice that the value is actually 28 decimal, even though, on a given target machine, it might be represented as its binary, octal, or hexadecimal equivalent. Consequently, all that is required is to subtract from it the ICC value of zero, which is 27, producing the digit 1. If this digit is multiplied by its own base, 10, as often as another digit is found in the scan, then the correct value will be obtained regardless of the base of the target machine. Consequently, when the scan encounters the value 30, the zero bias can be subtracted and the remainder added to the previously multiplied value.

If the original number, 13, had been keypunched in its octal representation, 015, then the BCD string 48, 49, 53 in BUFFER would have been translated to 27, 28, and 32 in the array SOURCE. By using the leading zero to indicate that the base is 8 instead of 10, the process reduces to that for decimal numbers.

The subroutine READ NUMBER illustrates this process. It is called only by Verb List E, the subroutine ADVANCE, and does not itself call any other subroutines. Operand Table B, which is not itself a part of the compiler, shows that while only two global variables are busy-on-entry to this subroutine, four of them are busy-on-exit.

The subroutine READ NUMBER, given in Verb List B, is based upon the assumption that it will only be called in cases in which the SOURCE pointer, I, is pointing at the leading digit, $\geqslant 0$, of a number, and that upon exit it should leave I pointing at the operator following the last digit. Techniques for testing the legality of the number are not shown, and Noun List B contains only those entries not previously defined in Noun List A.

Operand Table B

Operand	Class	Used in verb lists	Busy-on-entry	Busy-on-exit
O	Global constant	A,B,C,E,F,G,H,I,J,N	—	—
O1	Global constant	A,B,C,E,F,G,H,I,J,K,N	—	—
I	Global pointer	A,B,C,E,J,K,N	Yes	Yes
BASE	Local variable	B	No	No
DECIMAL BASE	Local constant	B	—	—
HEXIBASE	Local constant	B	—	—
ICC0	Global constant	B,C,K	—	—
NR FLAG	Global flag	B,C,E,G,J	No	Yes
NUMBER	Global variable	B,G,J	No	Yes
OCTAL BASE	Local constant	B	—	—
SOURCE	Global variable	A,B,C,E,J,K.	Yes	Yes

Noun List B

```
BASE,
DECIMAL BASE = 10,
HEXIBASE = 0010,
ICC 0 = 27,
NR FLAG,
NUMBER,
OCTAL BASE = 010;;
```

Verb List B

```
READ NUMBER: {
    O → NUMBER,
    O1 → NR FLAG,
    DECIMAL BASE → BASE,
    ICC 0 < SOURCE[I]:  TREAT DIGIT.;
        OCTAL BASE → BASE,
        I + O1 → I,
        SOURCE[I] < ICC 0:  EXIT NR.;  / / The number was zero.
        ICC 0 < SOURCE[I]:  TREAT DIGIT.;
            HEXIBASE → BASE,

NEXT DIGIT:
    I + O1 → I,
    SOURCE[I] < ICC 0:  EXIT NR. ; / / when an operator is reached.

TREAT DIGIT:
    NUMBER * BASE → NUMBER,
    NUMBER – ICC 0 → NUMBER,
    NUMBER + SOURCE[I] → NUMBER,
    NEXT DIGIT.

EXIT NR: }
```

A few examples may help to explain this procedure. First, assume that the Noun List B entry "DECIMAL BASE = 10," was itself being scanned, and the array SOURCE contained the ICC representation in octal, representing that declaration.

I	SOURCE[I]
0	50
1	51
2	47
3	55
4	61
5	45
6	60
7	46
8	45
9	67
10	51
11	10
12	34
13	33
14	1

Note that while there were embedded blanks in the declaration itself, these would have been removed by Verb List A, when it filled the array SOURCE. (To test the accuracy of the entries above, one can check against Table 4.1, p. 18). Now if we assume that the subroutine is called when a literal number is encountered, we will have the global pointer $I = 12$, pointing at the digit 1, represented by the value 34 in SOURCE[12]. Examining the algorithm, we see the BASE will be set to a decimal 10, and since 033 < 034, it will not be reset. Instead, control will pass immediately to TREAT DIGIT. The first time that this loop is entered, NUMBER will have been set to zero, hence multiplying by BASE will not change it. For our example, we will have

$$0 - 033 + 034 = 1$$

in NUMBER before returning to NEXT DIGIT, where the pointer I will be increased to 13. Then SOURCE[13] = 033, and since this is not less than ICC0 = 033, the symbol must represent another digit. At this point, then, we obtain:

$$1 \times 10 - 033 + 033 = 10$$

in the word NUMBER. Upon returning to NEXT DIGIT, where I becomes 14, we have SOURCE[14] = 1. Since this is less than ICC0 = 033, I is pointing at the next operator, a comma, and the procedure is complete.

As a second example, consider the case which would have arisen if the previous declaration had been expressed in the perfectly correct form "DECI-MAL BASE = 012,." The final content of NUMBER would then have been:

$$1 \times 8 - 033 + 035 = 10.$$

Hence the value is, as it should be, the same in either case. Note that while the value is shown to a decimal base, this places no restriction upon the representation within the computer registers, where it can obviously be held in base two. This fact assures us that the algorithm will not need modification to accommodate, say, a decimal machine.

But before keypunching this subroutine as it stands, and then programming it in the selected language, one should consider whether any other peculiarities of the target machine would require special attention. Is there any danger that numbers as large as those used in the noun list would not be handled correctly by your target machine? This should be expected if the machine has floating point, but not integer, multiplication.

After the basic compiler is self-compiling, it would be of value to return to this subroutine and consider how it might be extended to handle floating-point numbers. Would the presence of a decimal point (or period) in the number provide a sufficient clue to the extended subroutine? Could the noun list specifications be extended in such a way that, in the following example,

$$A = 10,$$
$$B,$$
$$C.$$
$$D = 10.0;$$

the first two entries are typed as fixed point, while both C and D are detected to have an OPERAND TYPE of floating point?

Reference

Knuth, D. *The Art of Computer Programming*, vol. 2, *Seminumerical Algorithms*, Reading, Mass.: Addison-Wesley, 1971.

Chapter 7

Hashing Symbol Tables

If there is even one universally accepted principle in assembler or compiler implementation, it is that symbol tables should be handled with the technique called *hash coding* or *scatter storage addressing*. On the other hand, there is much less unanimity regarding which particular variant of the method is to be preferred. Consequently, the example to be illustrated will be as simple as possible in order that, once the basic compiler is self-compiling, interesting experiments may be made by substituting more complex algorithms and measuring their effect on compiling times.

Hash coding, in its basic form, uses some computable function of the numeric representation of a name to determine at which point in a list the name should be entered. A search for a name in the list then reduces to recalculating the function and examining the entry at the calculated location. Since the table space is almost always much less than the possible name space, the function is normalized to the table size. Since more than one name may then yield the same index, the possibility of *collisions* must be handled. In the subroutine READ NAME, or Verb List C, collisions are handled with a linear search, and it is assumed for simplicity that while the table is circular, there will never be an actual table overflow.

While the subroutine, READ NUMBER, in Chapter 6 handled only the single task of converting from internal compiler code (ICC) in the source string to a value in the word NUMBER, the subroutine READ NAME must handle several duties. These may be listed as:

1. Scan each character in a name of any length, stopping with the source pointer I aimed at the first operator following the name.
2. Pack the first six characters of the name, in ICC, into the word NAME, and ignore any following characters.
3. Calculate arithmetically an index value for the name, based upon the numerical equivalent of its first six characters.
4. Determine whether the name has previously been entered in the symbol table list called NAME LIST. If it has, place the corresponding entry

31

from the parallel list NAME LOCATION in the word ADDRESS. If, instead, it is a newly encountered name which has not yet been entered into NAME LIST, do not enter it, but maintain the point at which it would be entered in the global pointer *N*.

5. Set the flag NAME FOUND to zero if it was not already in the list, or to 1 if it was.
5. Finally, test to determine whether an address beyond memory has already been assigned to the name. If so, this indicates that a declaration of the form NA:NR has been used in a special way involving crutch coding, and that the address will be needed in the word NUMBER. (This technique will be explained later, in the section on EQUIVALENCE in Verb List G [p. 46] and the section on Machine Language in Verb List J [p. 57].)

The subroutine READ NAME is called by the three subroutines ADVANCE, BUILD SUBROUTINE, and INITIALIZE LISTS, but it does not itself call any other subroutines. As can be seen in Operand Table C, this subroutine employs some 19 operands, 4 of which are busy-on-entry, and 10 busy-on-exit.

Operand Table C

Operand	Class	Used in verb lists:	Busy-on-entry	Busy-on-exit
O	Global constant	A,B,C,E,F,G,H,I,J,N	—	—
O1	Global constant	A,B,C,E,F,G,H,I,J,K,N	—	—
O100	Local constant	C	—	—
I	Global pointer	A,B,C,E,J,K,N	Yes	Yes
N	Global pointer	C,D	No	Yes
ADDRESS	Global variable	C,E,F,G,I,J,K,L	No	Yes
BYTE SIZE	Local constant	C	—	—
ICCO	Global constant	B,C,K	—	—
MAX ADDRESS	Global constant	C,G	—	—
MAX NAME	Local constant	C	—	—
NAME	Global variable	C,D,H,I	No	Yes
NAME FOUND	Global flag	C,J	No	Yes
NAME LIST	Global variable	C,D,N	Yes	Yes
NAME LOCATION	Global variable	C,D,M	Yes	Yes
NAME SPACE	Global constant	C,N	—	—
NR FLAG	Global flag	B,C,E,G,J	No	Yes
NUMBER	Global variable	B,C,G,J	No	Yes
SCATTER	Local variable	C	No	No
SOURCE	Global variable	A,B,C,E,J,K	Yes	Yes

Declarations which are used for the first time by Verb List C are given in Noun List C. Two points should be noted. First, the value of MAX NAME has been given a value which will provide that only the first six characters of a name are retained. While this is reasonable for a computer with 36-bit words, it may need to be altered to take advantage of a different word size.

Second, the value of NAME SPACE has been set at 512 decimal or 1000 octal, which is adequate to compile a program as large as the compiler. While it may be altered, care should be exercised, since most hashing schemes require a symbol table length which is equal to a power of two.

Noun List C

```
ADDRESS,
BYTE SIZE = 0100,
MAX ADDRESS = 0200000,
MAX NAME = 010000000000,
NAME,
NAME FOUND,
NAME LIST[512],
NAME LOCATION[512],
NAME SPACE = 512,
O100 = 0100,
SCATTER; ;
```

In addition to calculating the scatter index and determining whether a given name has already been entered in the array NAME LIST, the subroutine READ NAME will, if it finds a match, transfer the corresponding entry from the parallel array NAME LOCATION to the word ADDRESS. At this point one may begin to see how the remaining subroutines must operate, and it might be helpful to note that just as the global index I is being used as a pointer to the source code, the index J is a pointer to the object code as it is generated, and the index N is used as a pointer to a name's position in the symbol table.

Verb List C

```
READ NAME: {
    SOURCE[I] → NAME,
    NAME * O100 → SCATTER,
MORE NAME:
    I + O1 → I,
    SOURCE[I] < ICC 0:  SEARCH NAME LIST.;
        NAME < MAX NAME:  ADD CHARACTER.;
            MORE NAME.
ADD CHARACTER:
    NAME * BYTE SIZE → NAME,
```

```
      NAME + SOURCE[I] → NAME,
      NAME + SCATTER → SCATTER,
      MORE NAME.
  SEARCH NAME LIST:
      O → NAME FOUND,
      SCATTER/ NAME SPACE → N,
      N * NAME SPACE → N,
      SCATTER – N → N,
  TEST ENTRIES:
      NAME = NAME LIST[N]:   FOUND.;
         O = NAME LIST[N]:   EXIT RN.;
            N + O1 → N,
            N < NAME SPACE:   TEST ENTRIES.;
               O → N,
               TEST ENTRIES.
  FOUND:
      O1 → NAME FOUND,
      NAME LOCATION[N] → ADDRESS,
      ADDRESS < MAX ADDRESS:   EXIT RN.;
         ADDRESS – MAX ADDRESS → NUMBER,
         O1 → NR FLAG,
  EXIT RN: }
```

In this subroutine, do you see how a long name may be *read*, but only the first six characters *remembered?* Could you change this by providing a new value for MAX NAME? How might you modify the program to use 14-character names on a 16-bit machine? Is it apparent that this subroutine will leave the index *I* pointing to an operator when it exits? While it would appear that it should never be called unless *I* was pointing to the first *letter* of a legal name, might it also be capable handling an internally generated name such as $0000?

At this point do not be too concerned about the role of the variable MAX ADDRESS. It serves a function only when the assembly language mnemonics of any target machine are to be used in crutch coding, and will be discussed in later sections.

Since the actual entry of a name in the name list will not invariably follow immediately upon reading a name that is not already in the list, a separate subroutine Verb List D is used to insert it at a later time.

The subroutine NAME DEFINITION, given in Verb List D, is called by the four different subroutines COMP DECLARATIONS, COMP VERB LIST, BUILD SUBROUTINE, and INITIALIZE LISTS. The subroutine NAME DEFI-NITION calls the subroutine FILL FORWARD REFERENCES, which may also call the subroutine BUILD COMMAND. It uses only the five variables shown in Operand Table D.

Operand Table D

Operand	Class	Used in verb lists	Busy-on-entry	Busy-on-exit
J	Global pointer	D,F,G,H,I,J,K,M,N	Yes	Yes
N	Global pointer	C,D	Yes	No
NAME	Global variable	C,D,H,I	Yes	No
NAME LOCATION	Global variable	C,D,M	No	Yes
NAME LIST	Global variable	C,D,N	No	Yes

Since Verb List D does not use any new declarations, we do not need a separate noun list for it. The function of NAME DEFINITION, in addition to inserting a name in the symbol table and passing its object program location, J, to the table, requires a call upon FILL FORWARD REFERENCES to handle the possibility that the name is that of a label previously encountered in a transfer statement.

Verb List D

```
NAME DEFINITION: {
    FILL FORWARD REFERENCES,
    NAME → NAME LIST[N],
    J → NAME LOCATION[N], }
```

The problem posed by forward references will be examined on pages 49–52, as will the calculation of the object program pointer J (see p. 44).

In performing later experiments with different methods of calculating the hash-coding index, the method described by Bell and Kaman should be used as a standard of comparison.

References

Bell, James R. and Kaman, Charles H. A linear quotient hash code. *Comm. Assoc. Computing Machinery* 13:675, 1970.

Hopgood, F. R. A. and Davenport, J. The quadratic hash method when the table size is a power of 2. *Computer Journal* 15:314, 1972.

Chapter 8

The Basic Scan

Having developed the subroutines for reading cards, names, and numbers in the preceding sections, it is now a simple task to scan the source string. The objective is to obtain the next operator-operand-operator combination for use in analyzing either a noun list or a verb list.

The subroutine ADVANCE, or Verb List E, is called by the two subroutines COMP DECLARATIONS and COMP VERB LIST, and may call each of the three subroutines NEXT CARD, READ NAME, and READ NUMBER. It uses the 12 operands shown in Operand Table E.

Operand Table E

Operand	Class	Used by verb lists	Busy-on-entry	Busy-on-exit
O	Global constant	A,B,C,E,F,G,H,I,J,N	—	—
O1	Global constant	A,B,C,E,F,G,H,I,J,K,N	—	—
I	Global pointer	A,B,C,E,J,K,N	Yes	Yes
ADDRESS	Global variable	C,E,F,G,I,J,K,L	No	Yes
CURRENT OP	Global variable	E,J	No	Yes
LAST CHAR POINTER	Global pointer	A,E,N	Yes	Yes
LAST NUMBER	Local constant	E	—	—
LAST OPERATOR	Local constant	E	—	—
NR FLAG	Global flag	B,C,E,G,J	No	Yes
NEXT OP	Global variable	E,G,J	Yes	Yes
OPERAND TYPE	Global flag	E,J	No	Yes
SOURCE	Global variable	A,B,C,E,J,K	Yes	Yes

Only five of the operands used in ADVANCE have not previously been defined, and they are given in Noun List E. The global flag OPERAND TYPE has a rather limited role in the basic Pilot compiler, but this would change as the language is extended to handle literals, part words, and floating-point variables.

Noun List E

CURRENT OP,
LAST NUMBER = 36,
LAST OPERATOR = 26,
NEXT OP,
OPERAND TYPE;;

In addition to advancing the scanning process to the next combination of an operator-operand-operator triple occurring in the source string, the subroutine ADVANCE must also obtain the information about the operand which the routine calling it will need. This is accomplished by the call upon the subroutine READ NAME, which not only scans an operand, but obtains the location in memory to which it has been assigned, and stores this datum in word AD-DRESS.

The subroutine itself, as given in Vert List E, is always called with the global pointer I aimed at the operator in the source string which had already been transferred to the variable NEXT OP when it had scanned the preceding triple. When the pointer is advanced by one, simple tests of the numerical internal compiler code (ICC) value of the character pointed at will determine whether it is a letter, a digit, or another operator. In the latter case, the operand member of the triple is null, and must be so reported. In case a digit has been reached, a number has been encountered, and the subroutine READ NUMBER will complete the scan. Since literals are not legal in basic Pilot verb lists, this will occur only in noun lists, until such time as an implementor extends his language. If ADVANCE encounters a letter, then it assigns the task of continuing the scan to READ NAME, as noted earlier.

Verb List E

ADVANCE: {
    NEXT OP → CURRENT OP,
    O → ADDRESS,
    O → NR FLAG,
    O → OPERAND TYPE,
    I + O1 → I,

READVANCE:
    1 < LAST CHAR POINTER: NEW OPERAND.;
    NEXT CARD,
    READVANCE.

NEW OPERAND: // Is Source[I] a letter, a number, or operator?
    LAST NUMBER < SOURCE[I]:   GET NAME.;
        LAST OPERATOR < SOURCE[I]:   GET NUMBER.;
        FILL NEXT OP.

GET NAME:
  O1 → OPERAND TYPE,
  READ NAME,
  FILL NEXT OP.

GET NUMBER:
  O1 → OPERAND TYPE,
  READ NUMBER,

FILL NEXT OP:
  SOURCE[I] → NEXT OP, }

In the preceding algorithm, do you see what will happen in case there is no operand between two operators, as between the period and semicolon terminating a comparison? How is this information passed to the calling routine?

Does the current operator—next operator (CO—NO) combination suggest how a single operator is able to be used in more than one way, as the colon is in labels and in comparisons? This point will be expanded in Chapter 11.

Chapter 9

Compiling Declarative Statements

In compiling the declarative statements or noun list of a program, it will be necessary to insert initial values of some variables directly into the data area of the object program being generated. Later, when compiling the executable statements, or verb list of a program, it will also be necessary to insert material (operation codes and operand addresses) directly into the object program. While the material inserted in these two cases is clearly quite different, there is a definite advantage to be gained by having all insertions into the object program performed by a separate subroutine. With this approach, errors in the compiler will be easier to detect and eliminate than would be the case if each generator were written to make its own insertions independently. In at least one large and complex compiler which had not included this design criteria, it eventually became necessary to redesign in order to include it.

In the Pilot compiler, this subroutine is called BUILD COMMAND. While it is quite short, it is also quite machine-dependent. In the instance shown in Verb List F, it is based upon the fact that the target machine has a word structure providing for one operation code, one index register designator, and one operand address in each word. It will require alteration if it is to be adapted to a computer which has more than one instruction per word, or a computer that permits operand addresses to occupy alternate full words.

The subroutine BUILD COMMAND is called by the five subroutines COMP DECLARATIONS, FILL FORWARD REFERENCES, COMP VERB LIST, BUILD SUBROUTINE, and END SUBROUTINE, but it does not itself call any subroutines. It is called with the global pointer J indicating the next cell in the object program being compiled, and its function is to add the contents of ADDRESS, INDEX, and OP CODE, insert the sum into the object program at point J, and increment J. Since not all operands need be indexed, the value of INDEX must always be cleared after use, so this required action is performed here. This subroutine uses only the seven operands listed in Operand Table F.

While four of the five subroutines which call BUILD COMMAND use it in the standard way, COMP DECLARATIONS does not. Instead, it will be concerned with inserting single values, rather than assembling instructions, but it can still

Operand Table F

Operand	Class	Used by verb lists	Busy-on-entry	Busy-on-exit
O	Global constant	A,B,C,E,F,G,H,I,J,N	—	—
O1	Global constant	A,B,C,E,F,G,H,I,J,K,N	—	—
J	Global pointer	D,F,G,H,I,J,K,M,N	Yes	Yes
ADDRESS	Global variable	C,E,F,G,I,J,K,L	Yes	Yes
INDEX	Global variable	F,J,	Yes	No
OP CODE	Global variable	F,G,I,J,K,L	Yes	No
TEMP	Local variable	F,J	No	No

use BUILD COMMAND to do this, simply by putting the required value in one of the three words which are summed, and zeroing the other two.

The three new variables given in Noun List F are required. INDEX, which holds an index-designator bit, will be set in Verb List J to a value positioned in such a way that the parts of the word corresponding to the address field and to the function code of an instruction word are zeros. Similarly, Verb List J will set a value into OP CODE so that the parts of the word corresponding to both the index field and to the operand address field of an instruction word are zeros. Consequently, there will be no overlap when the three items are added together, just as though they had been logically "or'ed."

Noun List F

INDEX,
OP CODE,
TEMP;;

The second assignment in BUILD COMMAND makes use of the previously discussed ability of the language to address any word in memory specifically. While this capability is sometimes described as *direct addressing* when present in a higher-level language, it is really the same as the hardware feature called *indirect addressing* invented long ago by Heinz Schecher in Munich.

Verb List F

```
BUILD COMMAND: {
    OP CODE + INDEX → TEMP,
    TEMP + ADDRESS → [J],
    O → INDEX,
    J + O1 → J, }
```

All of the subroutines which will be required in compiling declarative statements or noun lists have now been examined, and we may proceed to the task itself. Looking back at Table 3.1 (see p. 14), or merely examining the previous noun lists, one can see the nature of the problems which must be solved.

The major functions of the subroutine COMP DECLARATIONS are:

1. For each variable named in a noun list, allocate a word in the object program for it, enter the name in the array NAME LIST for later use by the compiler, and enter the object program location allocated to it in the array NAME LOCATION, also for later use by the compiler.
2. For each variable which is an array, reserve the required space for it in the object program.
3. For each variable, including arrays, for which the source program specifies initial values, insert these values into the object program.
4. For each variable which has a synonymous or equivalent definition, (as expressed by a colon following the variable name), examine the synonym. If it is another name, assign it to the same location allocated to the original variable, and enter it in the NAME LIST and NAME LOCATION tables. If it is a number, use that number instead of the compiler assigned location as the location allocated to the variable in the object program.

The 19 operands used by COMP DECLARATIONS are given in Operand Table G.

Operand Table G

Operand	Class	Used in verb lists	Busy-on-entry	Busy-on-exit
O	Global constant	A,B,C,E,F,G,H,I,J,N	—	—
O1	Global constant	A,B,C,E,F,G,H,I,J,K,N	—	—
J	Global pointer	D,F,G,H,I,J,K,M,N	No	Yes
K	Local pointer	A,G,I,	No	No
ADDRESS	Global variable	C,E,F,G,I,J,K,L	No	Yes
COLON	Local constant	G	—	—
COMMA	Global constant	G,J	—	—
CURRENT OP	Global variable	G,E,J	No	Yes
DIAGNOSTIC	Global variable	G,J	No	No
EQUAL	Local constant	G	—	—
LEFT BRACKET	Local constant	G	—	—
MAX ADDRESS	Global constant	C,G	—	—
NEXT LOCATION	Global pointer	G,K,M	Yes	Yes
NEXT OP	Global variable	E,G,J	No	Yes
NR FLAG	Global flag	B,C,E,G,J	Yes	Yes
NUMBER	Global variable	B,C,G,J	Yes	Yes
OP CODE	Global variable	F,G,I,J,K,L	No	Yes
RIGHT BRACKET	Local constant	G	—	—
SEMICOLON	Local constant	G	—	—

Variables, constants, and arrays which have not previously been defined, but will be needed by the subroutine COMP DECLARATIONS are given in Noun List G.

Noun List G

```
COLON = 2,
COMMA = 1,
DIAGNOSTIC[14],
EQUAL = 8,
INDEX,
LEFT BRACKET = 11,
NEXT LOCATION,
OP CODE,
RIGHT BRACKET = 16,
SEMICOLON = 14,
TEMP;;
```

The variable NEXT LOCATION will be used as a global pointer to the cell in the data area being generated which is available to be allocated to a variable or the first value of an array. Its value varies from the value of the global pointer J only in those cases in which a <FILLED ARRAY> is being compiled. In addition to this use in compiling declarations, NEXT LOCATION will still be available later when a *program area* is being compiled, so that any transfer addresses which are modified by the program at run time may be stored in the *data area* instead of in the *program area*. If this is done, then reentrant code (*pure procedure*) will be generated, and more than one program can use the same code, or program area, at the same time provided only that each has its own data area.

The subroutine COMP DECLARATIONS is written in such a way that it must find two consecutive semicolons in order to exit correctly. This is done for only one reason, that of easing the task of extending the language, should any implementor eventually decide to do so. If it were desirable to add *block structure* to the language, then it might also be desirable to have the ability to specify one group of declarations as global, and a second group as local. The first semicolon would then separate the two groups and the second semicolon would terminate the noun list.

Verb List G

```
COMP DECLARATIONS: {
    0 → OP CODE,              // Clear so that BUILD COMMAND may be used.
    COMMA → NEXT OP,          // Initialize
CONT DECLARATIONS:
    ADVANCE,                  // Obtain another CO-OPERAND-NO triple.
```

```
        CURRENT OP = RIGHT BRACKET: CONT DECLARATIONS.;
         CURRENT OP = SEMICOLON: TEST TWO.;
           CURRENT OP = LEFT BRACKET: TEST ARRAY.;
            CURRENT OP = EQUAL: TEST INITIAL.;
            CURRENT OP = COLON: EQUIVALENCE.;
             CURRENT OP = COMMA: USE NO.;
               FAULT.
   TEST TWO:  // End of Noun List.
     NEXT OP = SEMICOLON: EXIT CD.;
       FAULT.

   TEST ARRAY:
     NEXT OP = RIGHT BRACKET: SET ARRAY SIZE.;
       FAULT.

   TEST INITIAL:
     NEXT OP = COMMA: INITIAL VALUE.;
     NEXT OP = SEMICOLON: INITIAL VALUE.;
       FAULT.

   USE NO:
     NEXT OP = EQUAL: NEW NAME.;
       NEXT OP = LEFT BRACKET: NEW NAME.;
         NEXT OP = COMMA: TEST NEW NAME.;
           NEXT OP = SEMICOLON: TEST NEW NAME.;
             NEXT OP = COLON: NEW NAME.;
               FAULT.
   TEST NEW NAME:
     NR FLAG = O1: INITIAL VALUE.;
       NEW NAME.

   DONT ADVANCE:                          // A synonym has been found.
     NEXT LOCATION - O1 → NEXT LOCATION,

   NEW NAME:
     NEXT LOCATION → J,
     NAME DEFINITION,
     NEXT LOCATION + O1 → NEXT LOCATION,
     CONT DECLARATIONS.

   INITIAL VALUE:
     NUMBER → ADDRESS,
     BUILD COMMAND,
     CONT DECLARATIONS.

   SET ARRAY SIZE:                        // Do not yet advance J, for there
                                          // may be initial values.

     J + NUMBER → NEXT LOCATION,
     CONT DECLARATIONS.

   EQUIVALENCE:                           // Either a synonym, or a programmer-
                                          // specified address.

     NR FLAG = O: DONT ADVANCE.;
       MAX ADDRESS + NUMBER → J,
```

```
    NEXT LOCATION - O1 → NEXT LOCATION,
    NAME DEFINITION,                    // Replace the compiler generated
                                        // address with the programmer-
                                        // specified one.
    CONT DECLARATIONS.
FAULT:
    O → K,
    CURRENT OP → DIAGNOSTIC[K],
    O1 → K,
    NEXT OP → DIAGNOSTIC[K],
    <DIAGNOSTIC>,
    CONT DECLARATIONS.
EXIT CD: }
```

Do you see why the standard object-code pointer, J, is augmented by the additional pointer NEXT LOCATION? Would this be required if the language being compiled did not permit the specification of initial values in declaration statements?

Reference

Schecher, Heinz. Massnahmen zur Vereinfachung von Rechenplänen bei elektronischen Rechenan; zeitschrift für angewandte Mathematik und Mechanik 36:377, 1956.

Chapter 10

Handling Forward References

Both assemblers and compilers must handle the problem which arises whenever the scan encounters a transfer to a label which has not yet been reached. In addition, compilers must provide either the same, or a similar mechanism for treatment of calls upon subroutines whose definitions do not precede the call. While the simplest solution for the implementor in either case involves making two passes over the program being translated, the resultant inefficiency is seldom warranted.

In the two subroutines, SAVE FORWARD REFERENCE and FILL FORWARD REFERENCES, this problem is handled by setting up two parallel arrays, TRANS NAME and TRANS LOCATION, to keep track of all such occurrences.

Verb List H, the subroutine SAVE FORWARD REFERENCE, is called only by the subroutine COMP VERB LIST, and does not itself call any subroutines. It makes use of the constants, variables and arrays shown in Operand Table H.

Operand Table H

Operand	Class	Used by verb lists	Busy-on-entry	Busy-on-exit
O	Global constant	A,B,C,E,F,G,H,I,J,N	—	—
O1	Global constant	A,B,C,E,F,G,H,I,J,K,N	—	—
J	Global pointer	D,F,G,H,I,J,K,M,N	Yes	Yes
L	Local counter	A,H,N	No	No
NAME	Global variable	C,D,H,I	Yes	Yes
TRANS COUNT	Global counter	H,I,N	Yes	Yes
TRANS LOCATION	Global variable	H,I	Yes	Yes
TRANS NAME	Global variable	H,I,N	Yes	Yes

This subroutine is called only when the subroutine ADVANCE, when called by COMP VERB LIST, has found an operand which has not yet been entered in the array NAME LIST. From the definition of the language, it follows that such

45

a name should be that of a label or subroutine not yet encountered in the compilation process.

Noun List H specifies the three additional variables required.

Noun List H

```
TRANS COUNT,
TRANS LOCATION[200],
TRANS NAME[200] ;;
```

Verb List H must place the name it receives in the array TRANS NAME[L], even though that particular name has already been entered elsewhere in the array, so that it may record the address in the object program, J, to which the current need applies in the parallel array TRANS LOCATION[L]. Since names are cleared from the array TRANS NAME by another subroutine when their definitions are found, SAVE FORWARD REFERENCES uses the rather clumsy approach of searching for the first empty cell in the list, in order to economize on needed list length. Clearly, a clever implementor might improve this subroutine by combining a hashing technique with chaining. It is recommended, however, that any such improvements be postponed until the basic version is completely checked out, because any increases in complexity have the usual effect of greatly amplifying the difficulty of detecting and eliminating errors. On the other hand, adding a test for list overflow to SAVE FORWARD REFERENCE would clearly fall in the realm of good programming practice.

Verb List H

```
SAVE FORWARD REFERENCE: {
    0 → L,
FIND EMPTY SLOT:
    TRANS NAME[L] = O: FILL SLOT.;
    L + O1 → L,
    FIND EMPTY SLOT.
FILL SLOT:
    NAME → TRANS NAME[L],
    J → TRANS LOCATION[L],
    L = TRANS COUNT: EXIT SFR.;
        TRANS COUNT + O1 → TRANS COUNT,
EXIT SFR: }
```

The subroutine FILL FORWARD REFERENCES, given as Verb List I, is called only by the subroutine NAME DEFINITION, and itself calls only BUILD COMMAND. It is called whenever the definition of a new operand has been obtained. Its function is to find all of those cases in which the address of the label or subroutine had been needed in an instruction previously generated. It does this by searching the list TRANS NAME, and obtaining corresponding addresses from the parallel list TRANS LOCATION.

This subroutine must then insert the address of the label or subroutine into the address field of the instruction which had previously been generated without it. It must also remove the name from the list of those needed, so that upon completion of the compilation process, it can be readily seen that the list TRANS NAME is indeed empty. In a more powerful system, however, if entries remained in the TRANS NAME list upon completion of compilation, they would be compared with the names of subroutines in the systems library before error messages were issued.

Operand Table I shows the constants and variables used by FILL FORWARD REFERENCES.

Operand Table I

Operand	Class	Used in verb list	Busy-on-entry	Busy-on-exit
O	Global constant	A,B,C,E,F,G,H,I,J,N	—	—
O1	Global constant	A,B,C,E,F,G,H,I,J,K,N	—	—
J	Global pointer	D,F,G,H,I,J,K,M,N	Yes	Yes
K	Local counter	A,G,I,N	No	No
ADDRESS	Global variable	C,E,F,G,I,J,K,L	No	Yes
NAME	Global variable	C,D,H,I	Yes	Yes
OP CODE	Global variable	F,G,I,J,K,L	No	Yes
TRANS COUNT	Global counter	H,I,N	Yes	Yes
TRANS LOCATION	Global variable	H,I	Yes	Yes
TRANS NAME	Global variable	H,I,N	Yes	Yes

As can be seen from Operand Table I, this subroutine does not make use of any nouns which have not previously been defined; hence, a separate noun list is not required.

Although we have seen how the subroutine BUILD COMMAND combines a value of OP CODE, INDEX, and ADDRESS and inserts them as an instruction word into the object code being generated, the way in which these items will be obtained will not be examined until Chapter 11. In the meantime, in order to understand the operation of FILL FORWARD REFERENCES, we need only assume that both OP CODE and INDEX were properly inserted, but that the address field was left blank. When the subroutine is called, the value of the global pointer J will be set to the location in the object program at which the next instruction would otherwise be generated. Accordingly, it represents the address to which the earlier transfer should be made. On the other hand, it also gives the location which the next call upon BUILD COMMAND would be expected to use. In order to maintain the design criteria that all entries in the object program be made via BUILD COMMAND, it is therefore necessary to both save the current value of *J* before replacing it with the location of the previously generated incomplete instruction, and to use it to set ADDRESS. Since the latter variable is not destroyed by BUILD COMMAND, it can serve both purposes simultaneously.

Since the language has neither the ability to specify bit fields nor the Boolean operator OR, that part of the previous instruction already generated is placed in OP CODE, so that BUILD COMMAND will add it to the newly determined address before overwriting the old instruction.

Verb List I

```
FILL FORWARD REFERENCES: {
    J → ADDRESS,                                    // also saves current value of J.
    O → K,
FILL ALL:
    TRANS COUNT < K: EXIT FFR.;
        NAME = TRANS NAME[K] : FILL LOCATION.;
        K + O1 → K,
        FILL ALL.
FILL LOCATION:
    O → TRANS NAME [K],                             // Clear the list entry.
    TRANS LOCATION[K] → J,
    [J] → OP CODE,
    BUILD COMMAND,
    K < TRANS COUNT: FILL ALL.;
        TRANS COUNT - O1 → TRANS COUNT,
EXIT FFR:
    ADDRESS → J, }
```

Examining both of the preceding subroutines, do you see why a program which included a large switch would compile faster if the switch followed, rather than preceded, the labeled points to which it referred? Could this point be generalized to show that the more a programmer knows about how any compiler he is using was implemented, the more efficiently he can use it?

An interesting and highly informative experiment may be performed later with the FORWARD REFERENCE subroutines, by designing a more sophisticated algorithm, and comparing its speed with the "brute force" approach illustrated. An appropriate chaining technique can be obtained from the reference cited.

Reference

Gear, C. William *Computer Organization and Programming*. New York: McGraw-Hill, 1969, especially pp. 338–340.

Chapter 11

Compiling with a CO—NO Table

The use of the current operator—next operator (CO—NO) table, often called a *transition matrix*, is both old and rather space-consuming, but it still appears to offer a basic advantage in speed of compilation, as well as ease of extension and straightforward error diagnostics. In addition to these tangible advantages, inherent in the CO—NO concept are several seldom-exploited capabilities which make them worthy of interest. Among the latter are their facility in allowing the overlapping and mixing of statement types, and their ability to provide a potential N * N unique operations from a character set of N operators. When one reflects upon the fact that the latter capability is basically the same as the *blending*, or combining of animal calls which, according to the anthropologists, helped produce the first human language, and then remembers that that device was invented by a bunch of prehistoric apes, it becomes obvious that the concept is neither new nor remarkably astute. Nevertheless, it will be used in the Pilot parser, which is the first part of the subroutine COMP VERB LIST.

In designing the CO—NO table (if one would do the task manually) the basic approach consists of setting up a matrix with operators ordered by the internal compiler code (ICC) across the top corresponding to current operator position, and along the side representing the next operator. Intersections of illegal (or unimplemented) CO—NO combinations are so marked, while legal pairs are set up as jumps to the appropriate generator. The approach is illustrated below, in which only a few of the set of operators are shown.

CURRENT OPERATOR

	ICC		0	1	2	3	4
		OP	.	,	:	→	+
	0	.	END or GOTO	GOTO	GOTO	X	X
NO	1	,	X	CALL	CALL	STORE	X
	2	:	LABEL	LABEL	X	X	X
	3	→	X	LOAD	LOAD	X	ADD
	4	+	X	LOAD	LOAD	X	X

In this example, only one combination presents ambiguity. Note that in a statement of the form:

$$Y \rightarrow ANSWER..$$

the presence a period as current operator and of a second period as next operator signals the end of a program. On the other hand, in a statement of the form:

$$ALTERNATIVE: POINT\ A.\ POINT\ B.\ POINT\ C.$$

a switch is implied, by means of which a statement:

$$O \rightarrow I,\ ALTERNATIVE[I].$$

would provide for transfer of control to the location of ALTERNATIVE plus zero, at which point an unconditional transfer to the location of a label, POINT A, should be generated. Similarly,

$$O1 \rightarrow I,\ ALTERNATIVE[I].$$

would provide for transfer of control to the instruction one word beyond the location of ALTERNATIVE, at which location a transfer to the location of the label POINT B would occur.

Both the end of a program and a switch are thus seen to use the same CO–NO combination. Consequently, the ambiguity must be resolved on the basis of whether the subroutine ADVANCE found an operand between the periods. As the table is expanded to include all possible operators, this technique can be used as needed.

Most compilers produce an intermediate n-address code, and many convert the intermediate code to assembly language output, but since Pilot itself so closely resembles 3-address code, and contains a simple assembler in its crutch-code feature, its output consists of absolute machine code.

Since the generators required are generally very simple, most of them are presented directly in the body of this subroutine. While all generators are inherently machine-dependent, they can nevertheless be written in higher-level language simply by storing the operation code values as constants in the noun list.

The function of the subroutine COMP VERB LIST, shown in Verb List J, therefore consists of parsing the imperative statements, piece by piece, and generating the appropriate object code. It is called only by the driver, COMPILE PILOT, and makes direct calls only upon the six subroutines ADVANCE,

BUILD COMMAND, BUILD SUBROUTINE, END SUBROUTINE, NAME DEF-
INITION, and SAVE FORWARD REFERENCES. It makes use of some 36
constants and variables, noted in Operand Table J.

Operand Table J

Operand	Class	Used in verb list	Busy-on-entry	Busy-on-exit
O	Global constant	A,B,C,E,F,G,H,I,J,N	–	–
O1	Global constant	A,B,C,E,F,G,H,I,J,K,N	–	–
O2	Local constant	J	–	–
I	Global pointer	A,B,C,E,J,K,N	Yes	Yes
J	Global pointer	D,F,G,H,I,J,K,N,M	Yes	Yes
M	Local pointer	A,J	No	No
AA	Machine code	J	–	–
ACTIVE	Local variable	J	No	No
ADDRESS	Global variable	C,E,F,G,I,J,K,L	Yes	Yes
ANA	Machine code	J	–	–
CODE SHIFT	Local constant	J	–	–
COMMA	Global constant	G,J	–	–
CURRENT OP	Global variable	E,J,G	Yes	Yes
DI	Machine code	J	–	–
DIAGNOSTIC	Global variable	G,J	No	No
DSA36	Machine code	J	–	–
ER	Machine code	J	–	–
INDEX	Global variable	F,j	No	Yes
INDEX SHIFT	Local constant	J	–	–
LA	Machine code	J	–	–
LMJB10	Machine code	J,L	–	–
LMJB11	Machine code	J	–	–
MSI	Machine code	J	–	–
NAME FOUND	Global flag	C,J	Yes	Yes
NEXT OP	Global variable	E,G,J	Yes	Yes
NR FLAG	Global flag	B,C,E,G,J	Yes	No
NR OF COS	Local constant	J	–	–
NUMBER	Global variable	B,C,G,J	Yes	Yes
OP CODE	Global variable	F,G,I,J,K,L	No	Yes
OPERAND TYPE	Global variable	E,J	Yes	No
SA	Machine code	J	–	–
SAVE D	Local variable	J	No	No
SOURCE	Global variable	A,B,C,E,J,K	Yes	Yes
SUB BIAS	Local constant	J	–	–
TEMP	Global variable	F,J	No	No
TG	Machine code	J	–	–
TNE	Machine code	J	–	–

In addition to the operation codes for the Univac 1108, Noun List J contains
a variable called ACTIVE, which is used in the only concession Pilot makes to

code optimization. It functions to prevent reloading a variable which is already available in the working register.

Noun List J

02 = 2,	
AA = 0140000000000,	// 1108 OP CODE — Add
ACTIVE,	
ANA = 0150000000000,	// 1108 OP CODE — Subtract
CODE SHIFT = 0100000000,	// To position Crutch-code mnemonics
DI = 0340000000000,	// 1108 OP CODE — Divide
DSA36 = 0732400000044,	// 1108 OP CODE — Shift before Divide
ER = 0724400000000,	// 1108 OP CODE — Interrupt to
	// Exec for I/O
INDEX SHIFT = 01000000,	// To position an index designator
	// in the proper field of an
	// instruction word.
LA = 0100000000000,	// 1108 OP CODE — Load
LMJB10 = 0745640000000,	// 1108 OP CODE — Transfer
LMJB11 = 0745660000000,	// 1108 OP CODE — SR CALL
MSI = 0310000000000,	// 1108 OP CODE — Multiply
NR OF COS = 10,	
SA = 010000000000,	// 1108 OP CODE — Store
SAVE D,	
SUB BIAS = 44,	// ICC FOR H
TG = 0550000000000,	// 1108 OP CODE — SKIP IF GREATER
TNE = 0530000000000;;	// 1108 OP CODE — SKIP IF NOT EQUAL

As the inclusion of the executive interrupt instruction, ER, implies, the simple input and output generators in the following subroutine depend upon the routines in the operating system, which will be examined later (see pp. 85–89). Since it is desirable to complete a compiler before embarking upon the operating system, it may be of advantage, at this point, to accept and adapt any I/O package readily available.

The subroutine COMP VERB LIST is the longest one in the compiler, but conceptually it is extremely simple. Immediately after calling the subroutine ADVANCE, it tests for the possibility that it has encountered an operand that is an undefined label or subroutine name. If so, it calls the subroutine SAVE FORWARD REFERENCE before proceeding. It then combines the ICC values of the current operator and the next operator to form an index into the transition matrix. The calculation itself is nothing more than *coding around* the lack of double subscripting in the language, but it should suggest one of the reasons for arranging the ICC of Chapter 4 to start with the operators, rather than with the numbers.

Logically, the matrix called CONO TABLE SWITCH should be placed immediately after the jump into it in the statement "CONO TABLE

SWITCH[M].", but consider the effect which this would have upon the compilation process. Since the switch itself contains 160 unconditional transfer statements to labels in this subroutine, it follows that if these are all forward references, the cost of treating them with both SAVE FORWARD REFERENCE and FILL FORWARD REFERENCES will be large. This cost may readily be avoided by the simple expedient of letting the switch follow the label definitions.

The remainder of Verb List J then consists of the various generators, which are discussed following their presentation.

Verb List J

```
COMP VERB LIST: {
        COMMA → NEXT OP,                         // Initialize for first call
                                                 // on ADVANCE
        NEXT CONO:
        ADVANCE,
            OPERAND TYPE = O: CALC CONO.;
                NAME FOUND = O1: CALC CONO.;
                    SAVE FORWARD REFERENCE,
CALC CONO:
        NEXT OP * NR OF CO S → M,
        M + CURRENT OP → M,
        CONO TABLE SWITCH [M].
// Switch follows generators for efficiency
TRY E:                                           // Either double period or switch
        OPERAND TYPE = O: EXIT CVL.;
            GO TO.
LABL:
        NAME DEFINITION,
        O → ACTIVE,
        NEXT CONO.
NOOP:
        COMMA → NEXT OP,
        NEXT CONO.
ML:                                              // Machine language
        ADVANCE,
        NUMBER * CODE SHIFT → OP CODE,
        ADVANCE,
        NR FLAG = O: INSERT CRUTCH CODE.;
            NUMBER → ADDRESS,
            BUILD INLINE CODE.
        INSERT CRUTCH CODE:
            NAME FOUND = O1: BUILD INLINE CODE.;
                SAVE FORWARD REFERENCE,
        BUILD INLINE CODE:
            BUILD COMMAND,
```

```
          COMMA → NEXT OP,
          NEXT CONO.
SS:                                          // Handle the subscript.
     OPERAND TYPE + O2 → OPERAND TYPE,
     I + O1 → I,
     SOURCE[I] – SUB BIAS → TEMP,
     TEMP * INDEX SHIFT → INDEX,
     I + O2 → I,
     SOURCE[I] → NEXT OP,
     CALC CONO,

GO TO:                                       // Generate a transfer.
     OPERAND TYPE = O: NEXT CONO.;
     LMJB10 → OP CODE,
     BUILD COMMAND,
     NEXT CONO,

CALL:                                        // Generate subroutine call.
     LMJB11 → OP CODE,
     BUILD COMMAND,
     O → ACTIVE,
     NEXT CONO.

LOAD:
     ADDRESS + INDEX → TEMP,
     TEMP = ACTIVE: LOADED.;
         TEMP → ACTIVE,
         LA → OP CODE,
         BUILD COMMAND,
         NEXT CONO.
     LOADED:
         O → INDEX,
         NEXT CONO,

TRY O:                                       // Either output or comparison
     O < OPERAND TYPE: LOAD.;
         O2 → ADDRESS,
     IO:
         ER → OP CODE,
         BUILD COMMAND,
         ADVANCE,
         O → OP CODE,
         BUILD COMMAND,
         COMMA → NEXT OP,
         O → ACTIVE,
         NEXT CONO.

TRY I:                                       // Either input or comparison
     O < OPERAND TYPE: LOAD.;
         O1 → ADDRESS,
         IO.

SREX:                                        // Subroutine exit
     END SUBROUTINE,
```

```
    COMMA → NEXT OP,
    O → ACTIVE,
    NEXT CONO.
DFSR:                                           // Define or open this SR.
    BUILD SUBROUTINE,
    COMMA → NEXT OP,
    NEXT CONO.
ADD:
    AA → OP CODE,
    BUILD COMMAND,
    NEXT CONO.
SUBT:
    ANA → OP CODE,
    BUILD COMMAND,
    NEXT CONO.
MULT:
    MSI → OP CODE,
    BUILD COMMAND,
    NEXT CONO.
DIV:                                            // Generate division.
    ADDRESS + INDEX → SAVE D,
    O → INDEX,
    O → ADDRESS,
    DSA36 → OP CODE,
    BUILD COMMAND,
    DI → OP CODE,
    SAVE D → ADDRESS,
    BUILD COMMAND,
    NEXT CONO.
STR:                                            // Generate store.
    SA → OP CODE,
    ADDRESS + INDEX → ACTIVE,
    BUILD COMMAND,
    NEXT CONO.
EQ:                                             // An equality comparison
    TNE → OP CODE,
    BUILD COMMAND,
    J + O2 → ADDRESS,
    GO TO.
LESS:                                           // A less-than comparison
    TG → OP CODE,
    BUILD COMMAND,
    J + O2 → ADDRESS,
    GO TO.
X:                                              // An error or an unimplemented
                                                // CO–NO

    O → M,
```

CURRENT OP→ DIAGNOSTIC[M],
O1 → M,
NEXT OP→ DIAGNOSTIC[M],
<DIAGNOSTIC>,
NEXT CONO,

CONO TABLE SWITCH:

//CO	.	,	:	→	+	−	*	/	=	<	
	TRYE.	GOTO.	GOTO.	X.	X.	X.	X.	X.	X.	X.	//NO=.
	X.	CALL.	CALL.	STR.	X.	X.	X.	X.	X.	X.	//NO=,
	LABL.	LABL.	LABL.	X.	X.	X.	X.	X.	EQ.	LESS.	//NO=:
	X.	LOAD.	LOAD.	X.	ADD.	SUBT.	MULT.	DIV.	X.	X.	//NO=→
	X.	LOAD.	LOAD.	X.	X.	X.	X.	X.	X.	X.	//NO=+
	X.	LOAD.	LOAD.	X.	X.	X.	X.	X.	X.	X.	//NO=−
	X.	LOAD.	LOAD.	X.	X.	X.	X.	X.	X.	X.	//NO=*
	X.	LOAD.	LOAD.	X.	X.	X.	X.	X.	X.	X.	//NO=/
	X.	LOAD.	LOAD.	X.	X.	X.	X.	X.	X.	X.	//NO==
	X.	TRYO.	TRYO.	X.	X.	X.	X.	X.	X.	X.	//NO=<
	X.	ML.	ML.	X.	X.	X.	X.	X.	X.	X.	//NO=$
	SS.	SS.	SS.	SS.	SS.	SS.	SS.	SS.	SS.	SS.	//NO=[
	X.	X.	DFSR.	X.	X.	X.	X.	X.	X.	X.	//NO={
	X.	SREX.	SREX.	X.	X.	X.	X.	X.	X.	X.	//NO=}
	NOOP.	X.	X.	X.	X.	X.	X.	X.	X.	X.	//NO=;
	X.	TRYI.	TRYI.	X.	X.	X.	X.	X.	X.	X.	//NO=>

EXIT CVL: }

Looking first at the CONO TABLE SWITCH, do you see how it has been compressed from the theoretically predicted $17^2 = 289$ entries to $16*10 = 160$ entries? Perhaps most obvious is the procedure used when subscripts are encountered. Since a subscript merely modifies the preceding operand, both left and right brackets can be treated and then "forgotten"; hence, neither needs to be passed along from the next operator position to the current operator position. Further, since the entire subscripting process is handled by a single generator, there is no need to enter the right bracket as even a next operator row in the matrix.

A less obvious form of reduction is possible whenever all of the entries for two different current operators are identical, as they may occasionally be for an unexpanded source language. For the case shown by the example, the semicolon is used only to suggest the possible expansion of a comparison statement to include both true and false sides of any form, including nesting to any depth. In the meantime, the semicolon in the current operator position behaves precisely as a comma. By converting all semicolons encountered as next operators to commas before passing them to the current operator position, the need for that row of the table is eliminated.

References

Halstead, M. H. *Machine-Independent Computer Programming.* Washington, D.C.: Spartan Books, 1962.

Huskey, H. D. Compiling techniques for algebraic expressions. *Computer Journal* 4:10, 1961.

Rosen, S. Spurgeon, R. A. and Donnelly, J. K. PUFFT, The Purdue University Fast Fortran Translator. *Comm. Assoc. Computing Machinery* 8:661, 1965.

For an interesting hypothesis on the original formation of human language, read the paper by anthropologists Charles F. Hockett and Robert Ascher, The human revolution. *American Scientist* 52:70, 1964, and note the striking similarity to the CO–NO table or transition matrix.

Chapter 12

Generating Reentrant Code

Consider a job using the compiler in a time-sharing environment which is interrupted before completion. The job which replaces the interrupted job may also use the compiler until it also is interrupted. Under these circumstances, if the code making up the compiler modifies itself in any way, such as saving a return address in the address field of an instruction, then it would be necessary to roll out the entire compiler when the first job was interrupted, and to save that copy of it until the first job was restored. The same condition would apply to the second job as well, and as many versions of the self-modified compiler as there were partially executed jobs would have to be stored. This requirement is avoided by generating reentrant code, often defined as *pure procedure*, which does not modify itself in any way. Clearly, this requires that even the *return address*, which must be saved at each subroutine call cannot be stored in the called routine, for that would imply modification. Neither can it be stored in a stack, as it could be for recursive subroutines, because there can be no assurance that the order of exit from a reentrant subroutine will bear any relation to the order of entry. Instead, it must be stored in the *data area*, with the space allocated to the noun list, since this area must in all cases be rolled out and saved with the individual job being interrupted.

In order to store this information in the data area, it is necessary to generate a name for each subroutine, and to allocate one word for it in the noun list. Because the name given to the subroutine by the programmer will already be in the name table, neither that name nor any other the programmer might use can serve this purpose. This presents a requirement for the compiler to be able to generate *illegal* names which may still be manipulated by its subroutines. Returning to Chapter 7 and examining the subroutine READ NAME, it is clear that the test for the alphanumeric property in each character of a name being read has been omitted for the first character, and that particular test has been left to the calling routine. Consequently, the subroutine READ NAME, if called by a routine other than ADVANCE, would also handle any name whose first character was an operator, provided that it could be assembling that name from the array SOURCE. Clearly, therefore, the compiler can generate and handle as many names of the form $000 through $999 as required, but just as clearly, it can not insert them into the 80-word array SOURCE, because that would destroy material being compiled. The solution to the latter problem lies in the fact that the compiler does not test indices for out-of-bounds conditions on array references. An additional array may therefore be set up, and provided only that the source pointer I is properly adjusted, READ NAME may read from it without being altered.

These processes are illustrated in the subroutine of Verb List K, BUILD SUBROUTINE. It uses the 14 operands listed in Operand Table K, and calls the subroutines READ NAME, NAME DEFINITION, and BUILD COMMAND. It is called by both the COMP VERB LIST and COMPILE PILOT subroutines.

Operand Table K

Operand	Class	Used in verb list	Busy-on-entry	Busy-on-exit
O1	Global constant	A,B,C,E,F,G,H,I,J,K,N	—	—
I	Global pointer	A,B,C,E,J,K,N	Yes	Yes
J	Global pointer	D,F,G,H,I,J,K,M,N	Yes	Yes
ADDRESS	Global variable	C,E,F,G,I,J,K,L	No	Yes
ICC O	Global constant	B,C,K	—	—
ICC A	Local constant	K	—	—
NEXT LOCATION	Global pointer	G,K,M	Yes	Yes
OP CODE	Global variable	F,G,I,J,K,L	No	Yes
SAVE I	Local variable	K	No	No
SAVE J	Local variable	K	No	No
SOURCE	Global variable	A,B,C,E,J,K	Yes	Yes
SR NR START	Local constant	K	—	—
SUBROUTINE LOCATION	Global pointer	K,L,M	No	Yes
SX	Machine code	K	—	—

The code which must be generated to handle both the calls upon subroutines, and the subroutine definitions themselves, must depend slightly upon the repertoire of instructions of the target machine, but the basic principles are the same in all cases. First, just before the actual transfer from the calling routine takes place, that routine must ascertain the address to which return will eventually be required and store that address in a place known to all subroutines, usually in one of the index registers of the computer. Then, the transfer to the first instruction in the subroutine may occur. In most machines, both these requirements are accomplished by a single instruction.

The first instruction in the subroutine must then transfer the return address to a safe place in the noun list, a place reserved for that particular subroutine. Subsequently, the last instruction in the subroutine must be a jump to the return address, which has been obtained from that safe place in the noun list. If the computer has *indirect* instructions, then, again, both obtaining the return address and transferring to it can be accomplished with a single instruction. In this case, the instruction will specify a transfer to the location in the noun list, but the indirect setting will cause the transfer of control to go instead to the location contained by that location.

The functions required of the subroutine BUILD SUBROUTINE may then be summarized as:

1. Bias the source pointer I to read a unique, compiler-generated name.
2. Bias the object code pointer J to point back to the end of the previously compiled noun list.
3. Allocate a cell in the noun list, and save the location of that cell for later use by the subroutine END SUBROUTINE.
4. Generate the first instruction in the subroutine, to store the return address.
5. Update the compiler-generated subroutine name so that a unique name will be available the next time that this subroutine is called.

Those operands which have not been defined in previous noun lists are given in Noun List K, and the routine itself is shown in Verb List K.

Noun List K

```
ICC A = 37,
SAVE I,
SAVE J,
SR NAME[5] = 10, 27, 27, 27, 1,          // Must follow SOURCE
SR NR START = 80,                         // For biasing to array
                                          // SOURCE

SUBROUTINE LOCATION,
SX = 010000000000;;                       // 1108 OP CODE-Store Call
                                          // Location
```

Verb List K.

```
BUILD SUBROUTINE: {
    I → SAVE I,
    SR NR START → I,
    J → SAVE J,
    NEXT LOCATION → J,
    NEXT LOCATION + 01 → NEXT LOCATION,
    READ NAME,
    NAME DEFINITION,
    J → ADDRESS,
    ADDRESS → SUBROUTINE LOCATION,
    SAVE J → J,
```

```
      SX → OP CODE,
      BUILD COMMAND,
STEP SR NUMBER:
      I - O1 → I,
      SOURCE[I] + O1 → SOURCE[I],
      SOURCE[I] < ICC A: RESTORE I.;
         ICC O → SOURCE[I],
         STEP SR NUMBER.
RESTORE I:
      SAVE I → I,}
```

In the preceding subroutine, the use of the single variable SUBROUTINE LOCATION to pass information to Verb List L, END SUBROUTINE, is only valid because of the rule that the definitions of subroutines cannot be nested. Note, however, that the only modification which would be required to remove this restriction on the language would be to replace the single variable with a push-down stack, SUBROUTINE LOCATIONS, indexed with a count of the depth of nesting. Note also that the process STEP SR NUMBER, which deals with characters in *internal compiler code* (ICC), is written so that it will perform a carry, and that the array SR NAME contains a final ICC comma to ensure termination of READ NAME.

Before adapting this subroutine to a different target computer, examine the complementary process, END SUBROUTINE, in Verb List L. The latter uses only those five operands given in Operand Table L, calls only the subroutine BUILD COMMAND, and is itself called only by the subroutines COMP VERB LIST and COMPILE PILOT.

Operand Table L

Operand	Class	Used in verb list	Busy-on-entry	Busy-on-exit
ADDRESS	Global variable	C,E,F,G,I,J,K,L	No	Yes
I BIT	Machine code	L	—	—
LMJB10	Machine code	J,L	—	—
OP CODE	Global variable	F,G,I,J,K,L	No	Yes
SUBROUTINE LOCATION	Global pointer	K,L,M	Yes	No

Since all other nouns have already appeared in earlier lists, Noun List L consists of a single entry, used to set the indirect field in an 1108 instruction.

Noun List L

I BIT = 0200000;;

Verb List L

```
END SUBROUTINE: {
    SUBROUTINE LOCATION + I BIT → ADDRESS,
    LMJB10 → OP CODE,
    BUILD COMMAND, }
```

Chapter 13

Driving the Compiler

Except for the need to initialize parameters and tables prior to a compilation run, all functions required to compile any source program have been completed in the previous sections. At this point, then, we may consider the requirements for a driver routine. For our example, this is quite simple, yet it does contain features which may not be obvious. First, when later incorporating the compiler into an operating system, it will be best that all programs, including the compiler itself, be compiled as subroutines, and have separate *data areas* and *code areas*. Since the language does not provide for nested subroutine definitions, this requires that the COMPILE PILOT subroutine *program around* the deficiency, accounting for four of the last five statements in Verb List M.

This subroutine calls the five subroutines INITIALIZE LISTS, COMP DEC-LARATIONS, BUILD SUBROUTINE, COMP VERB LIST, and END SUB-ROUTINE directly, and, indirectly of course, all of the others. While it is not itself called by any of its subroutines, it will be called by the operating system. It utilizes the operands given in Operand Table M, in which an asterisk in the third column indicates potential use or resetting by an operating system.

Operand Table M

Operand	Class	Used in verb list	Busy-on-entry	Busy-on-exit
J	Global pointer	D,F,G,H,I,J,K,M,N	No	Yes
NEXT LOCATION	Global pointer	G,K,M	No	Yes
NOUNS START	Local pointer	M,*	Yes	No
PROG LOCATION	Local pointer	M,*	No	Yes
PROG START	Local pointer	M,*	Yes	No
SUBROUTINE LOCATION	Global pointer	K,L,M	No	Yes

The functions which this highest-level subroutine must perform are simply those of initializing the pointers to the target language data area and program area, and calling a subroutine to initialize the compiler's own data area, another

63

to compile a noun list, and a third to compile a verb list. Before and after calling the latter—since any program to be compiled is to be treated as a subroutine whether it was written that way or not—it is necessary to invoke the appropriate routines directly, without waiting for them to be called by the subroutine ADVANCE.

Noun List M contains only the three previously undefined nouns shown, where the first and last have been given values corresponding to arbitrarily selected areas in core memory.

Noun List M

NOUNS START = 0120000,   // May be reset by operating system
PROG LOCATION,
PROG START = 030000;;   // May be reset by operating system

Verb List M

```
COMPILE PILOT: {
    NOUNS START → NEXT LOCATION,
    INITIALIZE LISTS,
    COMP DECLARATIONS,
    PROG START → J,
    BUILD SUBROUTINE,
    SUBROUTINE LOCATION → PROG LOCATION,
    COMP VERB LIST,
    PROG LOCATION → SUBROUTINE LOCATION,
    END SUBROUTINE, }
```

If it had been desirable to execute every source program as soon as it was compiled, without return to the operating system, then after the last statement in the preceding subroutine, one might have added the two statements:

PROG START → J,
[J].

Chapter 14

Initializing the Compiler

Aside from clearing lists and resetting counters, the initialization subroutine can be used to predefine any superglobal variables desired. In our example, the indices I through N are treated in this way, so that they will be available in any source program without the necessity for programmer definition. The technique used is quite similar to that employed in the reading of internally generated subroutine names in Verb List K, since here again an array, INDICES, is positioned after the array SR NAME, which follows immediately after SOURCE, in order that previously written procedures may be "tricked" into accepting it.

The function of the subroutine INITIALIZE LISTS may be stated quite simply as that of clearing the NAME LIST and TRANS NAME arrays, and predefining the indices. It calls upon the two subroutines READ NAME and NAME DEFINITION, and is itself called only by COMPILE PILOT. Operand Table N gives data on the 15 operands which it employs.

Operand Table N

Operand	Class	Used in verb list	Busy-on-entry	Busy-on-exit
O	Global constant	A,B,C,E,F,G,H,I,J,N	–	–
O1	Global constant	A,B,C,E,F,G,H,I,J,K,N	–	–
I	Global pointer	A,B,C,E,J,K,N	No	No
J	Global pointer	D,F,G,H,I,J,K,M,N	No	Yes
K	Global pointer	A,G,I,N	No	No
L	Global pointer	A,H,N	No	No
INDEX END	Local constant	N,*	–	–
INDEX NAME START	Local constant	N,	–	–
INDEX START	Local constant	N,*	–	–
LAST CHAR POINTER	Global pointer	A,E,N	No	Yes
NAME LIST	Global variable	C,D,N	No	Yes
NAME SPACE	Global constant	C,N	–	–
NR INDEXES	Local constant	N,*	–	–
TRANS COUNT	Global variable	H,I,N	No	Yes
TRANS NAME	Global variable	H,I,N	No	No
TRANS SPACE	Local constant	N	–	–

Here, as in Operand Table M, an * in the third column denotes the option of input from the operating system.

Noun List N contains all of the nouns required by the entire compiler which have not appeared in earlier lists. The value of INDEX NAME START is set at 85, so that when the three arrays–SOURCE[80], SR NAME[5] and IN-DICES[26]–are compiled contiguously, the 85 provides the proper bias for the source pointer I to reach the first word of the third array. The value of 111 for INDEX END is merely the sum of the lengths of the same three arrays. The third array contains the internal compiler code (ICC) representation of the name of each index, followed by a comma.

Noun List N

```
INDEX END = 111,                            // 80 + 5 + 26,
INDEX NAME START = 85                       // 80 + 5
INDEX START = 0,                            // May be reset by O.S.
INDICES[26] = 45, 1, 46, 1, 47, 1, 48, 1,
              49, 1, 50, 1, 52, 1, 53, 1,
              54, 1, 55, 1, 56, 1, 57, 1,
              58, 1,
NR INDEXES = 6,                             // May be reset by operating system
TRANS SPACE = 200;;                         // Array size in Noun List H.
```

As the preceding declarations suggest, in addition to the six indices I through N, provision is made for the set P through V. This is in order that we may have two modes of compilation, one for normal use and the second for compiling a more privileged operating system. Examine the following subroutine with that possibility in mind.

Verb List N

```
INITIALIZE LISTS: {
     0 → K,
     CLEAR NAME LIST:
     0 → NAME LIST[K],
     K + 01 → K,
     K < NAME SPACE: CLEAR NAME LIST.;
     0 → K,
     CLEAR FORWARD TRANSFERS:
     0 → TRANS NAME[K],
     K + 01 → K,
     K < TRANS SPACE: CLEAR FORWARD TRANSFERS.;
     0 → TRANS COUNT,
     INDEX NAME START → I,
     INDEX START → J,
     INDEX END → LAST CHAR POINTER,
     0 → L,
```

```
PREDEFINE INDEXES:
  READ NAME,
  J + O1 → J,
  NAME DEFINITION,
  I + O1 → I,
  L + O1 → L,
  L < NR INDEXES: PREDEFINE INDEXES.;
EXIT IL:
  O → I,
  O → LAST CHAR POINTER, }
```

Examining the starting value of J, and noting that it is not equal to NOUNS START minus 6 brings up an important point. Here the index registers on the machine are addressable. If a different target machine lacked this property, what differences would result in generating code for subscripted parameters? Assuming that that problem is solved, is there still another? Consider the difference between the two statements:

$$A[I] + B \to C,$$

and

$$I + B \to C,$$

and suggest how both uses of I might be treated.

At this point every part of the basic Pilot compiler has been detailed, and all of the steps outlined earlier in Fig. 1.3 (p. 7) should be ready for completion.

Extensions and modifications may be undertaken as soon as Version 1 has been debugged, or they may be delayed until the compiler has been incorporated into a basic time-slicing operating system. Clearly, no matter what its power, no compiler is more than half-completed until it has adequate error-detection capabilities. It might seem that the implementor of a self-compiler would be in a position to have personally encountered all of those points at which diagnostic messages might need to be generated, and while this is more nearly true for self-compilers than for those written in other languages, it is never completely so. After guarding against every error that one might make himself, it is alway surprising to note the completely new set of potential errors which arrives with the first group of users.

A list of more than 20 extensions can be found in Chapter 24, for use in the unlikely event that one has the basic compiler running before deciding upon the feature which he feels should be added first.

Chapter 15

Structural Design of a Time-Slicing Operating System

The complete time-sharing operating system described in the remaining chapters of this manual is an extremely minimal one. It has been designed and implemented solely to illustrate those features and techniques which appear basic to even the most simple system.

The functions which this system must perform include: (1) accepting and responding to control cards; (2) scheduling jobs from remote peripheral devices; (3) handling both input and output for differing types of readers or printers; (4) providing for the actions to be taken when either internal or external interrupts occur; (5) monitoring the time slices allocated to jobs; (6) saving and rolling out jobs whose current time slice is exhausted, and restoring them to execution status later. Further, it is written in such a way that it may slide into a machine being controlled by another operating system, and with proper manual intervention at the console, take control of the computer and eliminate the original operating system.

Because it is also written in the same language, it can be compiled by the Pilot compiler detailed in the previous chapters.

It is divided into the following ten routines and subroutines:

1. CONTROL CARD PROCESSOR
2. READ
3. PRINT
4. OUT MONITOR INTERRUPT
5. IN MONITOR INTERRUPT
6. ER (Executive Interrupt)
7. CLOCK
8. EXIT CK (Bypass day clock).
9. COLD START.
10. NEXT SLICE.

Because the system is driven by interrupts which may be generated by peripheral devices during the execution of any program, the standard type of flow-chart representation which may be used to describe an application program does not quite fit an operating system. Consequently, the flow chart shown in Fig. 15.1 must be interpreted with some care. It shows interrupt-initiated transfers of control with **dashed lines**, originating during execution of a user's program. While this is the normal course of events, it represents an oversimplification, because many parts of the operating system might themselves be in execution at the time an external interrupt occurs. While (as Chapter 16 will explain) the host machine has privileged instructions with which the operating system may inhibit or lock out interrupts, they can not be allowed to remain in effect during the entire time the operating system is in execution. A reason for this becomes clear if one considers a case in which all programs are *hung-for-IO* or suspended, pending completion of input requests. At that point, the operating system must remain in execution until it is notified, via an interrupt, that at least one of the input requests has been completed.

In the same way, one must be aware that the **double-headed dashed arrows** connected to routines 4, 5 and 8 merely indicate that upon completion of the instructions in any of those routines, control will be returned to the routine which was in execution when the interrupt occurred, no matter which one it was.

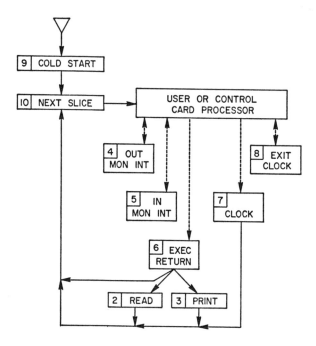

Fig. 15.1. Flow chart of the time-slicing operating system.

Another point which is not apparent from Fig. 15.1 concerns the way in which the Pilot compiler and the operating system are integrated. The fact that the operating system is written in the Pilot language (using crutch coding where indicated) makes it possible to compile it with the compiler, but this in itself does not make the compiler a part of the integrated system. In fact, the compiler must be put in a slightly special mode before compiling the operating system. This special mode consists only of providing 15, rather than 6, index registers, and basing them at a different address.

In order to combine these two basic parts of the total system, the following technique is used. First, a copy of the compiler developed in the previous chapters is compiled with NR OF INDEXES = 15 and INDEX START = 0. Then, an entire source deck of the standard compiler is included as a part of the routine CONTROL CARD PROCESSOR. As a result, when the operating system is compiled, it forms a self-contained unit, having both compiler and operating system.

References

Denning, P. Virtual memory. *Computing Surveys* 2:153, 1970.

Foster, Caxton C. An unclever time-sharing system. *Computing Surveys* 3:000, 1971.

Kilburn, T. Payne, R. B. and Howarth, D. J. "The Atlas Supervisor," in Saul Rosen, (ed.). *Programming Systems and Languages.* New York: McGraw–Hill, 1967, pp. 661–682.

Mealy, George H. "Operating Systems, Excerpts," in *Ibid.,* pp. 516–534.

PART II. OPERATING SYSTEMS

Chapter 16

The Host Machine

In the preceding chapters it was possible to explain and to understand the details of the compiler with virtually no knowledge of the specific computer upon which it operated, and with no resort to machine language or crutch coding. Without expanding the language, this is not feasible for the operating system. Not only will some 18 different machine language instructions be needed, but their use will be based upon the capabilities of the machine. Despite the fact that it may be possible to proceed as with the compiler, and ignore the details of the host machine as one devises solutions to the basic problems on one's own computer, the serious student is usually uneasy with that approach. Consequently, this chapter will be devoted to a discussion of those features of the host machine, the Univac 1108, which have a bearing upon the implementation of the example system, and those of its instructions which are used. Since this purpose will be served with an incomplete, and occasionally even oversimplified account, anyone interested in that computer per se should obviously consult the user's manual for it.

The 1108 is designed to operate in either of two modes, one for user programs and the other for executive or operating system routines. In the user mode, a group of *privileged instructions* are illegal, and only 47 of the 128 program-addressable, high-speed registers can be used. The mode is determined by the contents of an unaddressable register, the *processor state register* (PSR), which can be set by one of the privileged instructions, load PSR. The operating system is further protected by another unaddressable register, the *storage limits register* (SLR), set by another privileged instruction, load SLR. Pertinent details of these two registers will be shown later.

Each type of internally or externally generated interrupt transfers control to its own specific address in memory locations 136 through 167, and at the same time it changes the PSR to executive mode, and saves the previous content of the PSR in high-speed register O. The fixed-address assignments for those interrupts which are pertinent to the Pilot operating system are as follows:

71

Address		Interrupt
Decimal	Octal	
143	217	Day clock
144	220	Input monitor
145	221	Output monitor
153	231	Real-time clock
161	241	Illegal instruction
162	242	Executive return
163	243	Guard mode violation

Among the high-speed registers available in user mode, locations 1 through 15 are index registers, and locations 12 through 27 are accumulators. The four overlapping registers are dual purpose. In executive mode, there is a duplicate set of index registers and accumulators in locations 97 through 123.

Another group of high-speed control registers, also available only in executive mode, are *access control registers* for the 16 input-output channels. The input access control registers start at location 32 and continue through location 47. Locations 48 through 63 are the corresponding output control registers. Channel 15 is reserved for the control console.

The 1108 provides for fetching a current operand and the next instruction simultaneously, provided that they are located in different memory banks. Since this implies that instruction areas and data areas will be disjoint, the SLR provides for protection of both an instruction bank and a data bank while in the guard mode. The 36-bit SLR consists of four fields, each of which contains the high-order 9 bits of an 18-bit limiting address. (The low-order 9 bits are taken as zeros). The limiting addresses are entered as shown in Fig. 16.1.

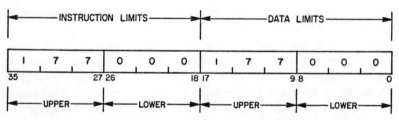

Fig. 16.1. The storage limits register (SLR).

As is shown in Fig. 16.1, the entire 65,000-word central memory would be unprotected. The limits of either the *instruction fields* or the *data fields* are tested against the address before any main storage reference, and an out-of-limits address generates an interrupt which returns control to the operating system.

The PSR is also a 36-bit register divided into four 9-bit fields, as shown in Fig. 16.2. This register controls the mode of the *central processing unit,* and contains

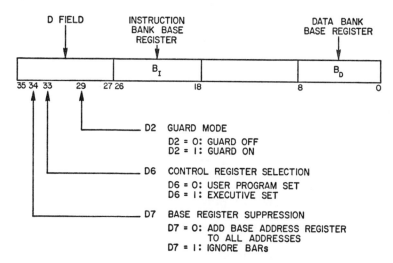

Fig. 16.2. The processor state register (PSR).

the *base address registers* (BAR) from which programs "float" in storage during execution. Individual bits of the D field determine the various modes. D2, or bit 29, determines the guard mode. With D2 = 0, instructions and storage references to the access control registers (locations 040 through 077), the real-time clock, (location 0100) and executive control registers (locations 0120 through 0177) are permitted. With D2 = 1, these are inhibited, and the contents of the SLR are also enforced.

D6, or bit 33, selects either of the two sets of control registers, one set for a user program, and a different set for the operating system. With D6 = 0, the user set, control registers 0 through 037 and 0100 through 0117 are available. When D6 = 1, the executive set, control registers at locations 0120 through 0177 are substituted. Furthermore, every occurrence of an interrupt automatically stores the contents of the PSR in cell zero, and then resets *D6* to 1.

D7, or bit 34, allows for suppression of BAR. With D7 = 0, the appropriate BAR (instruction or data, executive or user) is added to every address reference. When D7 = 1, the BAR are ignored.

The B$_I$ and B$_D$ fields of the PSR contain the high-order nine bits of the base addresses for instructions and data, respectively.

Most, but not all, of the 18 machine-language instructions required by the Pilot operating system are *privileged instructions,* which can be executed only in open, or unguarded mode. They are given in Table 16.1.

By using the preceding information to assist in following the routines and subroutines of the operating system described in subsequent chapters, it should be possible to find comparable capabilities either in the hardware, or by devising software substitutes, for a different target machine.

Table 16.1 Crutch-coded Machine language Instructions

Instruction	Effects
AACI	Allow all channel external interrupts and jump.
AAIJ	Allow all I/O interrupts and jump.
DIC	Disconnect input channel.*
DOC	Disconnect output channel.*
ER	Executive return. Causes the contents of the PSR to be stored at location zero, 1 → D6 and 1 → D7 of the PSR, and jumps to location 0242.
HJ	Halt and jump. Used as a stop.
JI	Jump indirect. Transfers control to the address stored at the location specified in the instruction.
JK1	Jump on key 1 set. Halts until key 1 on the console has been set, then transfers to the location given in the instruction.
LCR	Load channel select register.
LICM	Load input channel and monitor. Puts an access control word into the input access control register specified by the CSR, initiates input mode on that channel, and requests an interrupt upon completion.
LOC	Load output channel. The same as LOCM, except that monitoring does not occur.
LOCM	Load output channel and monitor. The same as LICM, except that *output* replaces *input.*
LPSI	Load processor state register, indirect. The address given in the instruction holds the address of the word to be loaded into the PSR.
LSL	Load storage limits register.
NOP	No operation.
PAIJ	Prevent all I/O interrupts and jump to address given in instruction.
SCN	Store channel number. Captures the active channel number and stores it at the address given in the instruction.
SLJI	Store location and jump indirect. The contents of the P register (program counter) minus the contents of the appropriate BAR is stored at the location pointed to by the contents of the address given in the instruction. Control is then transferred to that location plus one.

*The channel involved may be specified in the instruction, or held in a *channel select register* (CSR).

Reference

Univac 1108 Multi-Processor System, System Description. St. Paul, Minn.: Sperry Rand Corporation, 1968.

Chapter 17

Control Card Processing

The function of the *control card processor* is simply that of scanning a control card, determining the action required, and initiating that action. In the following example, only three control options are recognized: COMPILE, EXECUTE, and STOP. As a result, the processor itself should be most straightforward. In order to obtain an integrated system, however, the routine itself contains an entire Pilot compiler, so that it may perform compilation by calling one of its own subroutines. Thus, one might consider the control card processor as a part of the compiler. Accordingly, one should combine Noun List 1 with Noun Lists A through N, and insert a copy of the source decks of Verb Lists A through N directly ahead of the label EXECUTE:.

All the other components of the operating system (detailed in subsequent chapters) can then be treated as one separate program, and compiled ahead of the compiler. Both of these two major programs, OS and compiler, should be compiled with a version of the compiler for which INDEX START has been set to MONITOR INDEX START, and NR INDEXES has been set to 15.

Constants, variables, and arrays which have not previously been specified in Noun Lists A through N are given in Noun List 1.

Noun List 1

```
BCD C = 8,
BCD E = 10,
BCD S = 24,
CARD[14],
CC ERR MSG = 0 10 10 05 12 27 27,          // CC Ƀ ERR
06 = 6;;
```

In reading Verb List 1, it might be convenient to think of the subroutine called COMPILE PILOT with a more descriptive name, such as "Compile any source program written in the Pilot language."

Verb List 1

```
CONTROL CARD PROCESSOR:
  > CARD <,
  < CARD >,
  O1 → I,
  CARD[I] = BCD C: CALL COMPILER.;
    CARD[I] = BCD E: CALL EXECUTE.;
      CARD[I] = BCD S: STOP.;
        < CC ERR MSG >,
          CONTROL CARD PROCESSOR.
CALL COMPILER:
  OO → INDEX START,
  O6 → NR INDEXES,
  COMPILE PILOT,
  CONTROL CARD PROCESSOR.
CALL EXECUTE:
  EXECUTE,
  CONTROL CARD PROCESSOR.
COMPILE PILOT: {  }                              // Insert All of Pilot
EXECUTE: {
  PROG START → J, [J] . }
STOP: { .. }
```

In this routine, neither of the indices I or J are busy-on-entry, and are used only because the language requires the simple subscript structure.

Chapter 18

Controlling Input/Output

In this and the following sections, the index I is used as a pointer to the user. In addition to the console, which must be treated as a special case, there are assumed to be as many remote devices, each with its own I/O channel, as specified by the variable NR OF USERS. For the simple case, this will be set at 2.

The first set of declaration statements which are to be combined with following sets for the operating system are given in Noun List 2. The operands used by the routine READ, or Verb List 2, are shown in Operand Table 2.

Operand Table 2

Operand	Class	Used in verb list	Busy-on-entry	Busy-on-exit
I	Global pointer	2,3,6,7,9,10	Yes	Yes
J	Global pointer	2,3,4,5,6,7,9,10	Yes	Yes
ACCESS CONTROL	Local variable	2	No	No
CARD ACW	Local constant	2	—	—
CHAN SELECT	Global variable	2,3	No	No
CHAN TABLE	Global constant	2,3	—	—
CONSOLE	Global constant	2,3,5	—	—
RFCNACW	Local constant	2	—	—
TYPACW	Global constant	2,3	—	—
USER CORE OFFSET	Global constant	2,3,6	—	—

In Noun List 2, the channel number always assigned to the console, 15, should be the third entry in the array CHAN TABLE, but it also is needed separately. By holding the array to a length of two, and following it immediately by the single operand CONSOLE, both objectives are satisfied. The remote-user devices to be serviced are those assigned to channels 11 and 12.

The *access control word* (ACW) for the card reader must contain a word count of 80 decimal, or 120 octal, in bits 18 through 33, and leave space for later insertion of a *starting address* in bits 0 thru 17. Similarly, the ACW for the console typewriter must contain a count of 72 decimal, or 110 octal.

Noun List 2

```
ACCESS CONT,
CARDACW = 0120000000,                    // Word Count = 80.
CHAN TABLE[2] = 12, 11,
CONSOLE = 15,                            // Must follow CHAN TABLE
CHAN SELECT,
LCR: 0737000000000,                      // Load channel select register.
LICM: 0750400000000,                     // Load input channel and monitor.
LOC: 0752000000000,                      // Load output channel.
RFCNACW = 01000000000044,                // Device 044.
TYPACW = 0110000000,                     // Word count = 72.
USER CORE OFFSET[2] = 0110000, 0120000;; // Used to make
                                         // User IO buffer addresses
                                         // Absolute for IO.
```

In the following routine, Verb List 2 or READ, some four steps are involved. First, one must load the *channel select register* (CSR) with the value appropriate to the user. Second, one must construct the hardware transfer control word. This is done in two parts, the first of which makes use of the fact that the index *J* will have been set to the value of the program address counter by the *executive return interrupt* routine. The last part of this step depends upon whether the user was the console or not. If so, the proper bits are set. If not, the user was a remote device, so that in addition to setting the corresponding bits in the ACW, the appropriate "function" character required to specify a card read must be sent to the remote device.

The third step actually initiates the input transfer with an input monitor interrupt, and the last step returns to another part of the system for selection of the next ready user.

Verb List 2

```
READ:
    CHAN TABLE[I] → CHAN SELECT,
    $ LCR, CHAN SELECT;                          // Load channel select register.
    [J] + USER CORE OFFSET[I] → ACCESS CONT,
    CHAN SELECT < CONSOLE: READ REMOTE.;
        ACCESS CONT + TYPACW → ACCESS CONT,
        INPUT.

READ REMOTE:
    ACCESS CONT + CARDACW → ACCESS CONT,
    $ LOC, RFCNACW;                              // Send Function to CHANNEL.
INPUT:
    $ LICM, ACCESS CONT;                         // Load input channel and monitor
    NEXT SLICE.
```

The process for controlling printing, to be shown in Verb List 3 or PRINT, is quite similar, except that it must also translate from *internal compiler code* (ICC) to the appropriate output codes. The operands which it uses are given in Operand Table 3.

Operand Table 3

Operand	Class	Used in verb list	Busy-on-entry	Busy-on-exit
O1	Global constant	3,5,6,7,9,10	–	–
O3	Local constant	3	–	–
O4	Local constant	3	–	–
O110	Global constant	3,5	–	–
O240	Local constant	3,	–	–
I	Global pointer	2,3,6,7.9.10	Yes	Yes
J	Global pointer	2,3,4,5,6,7,9,10	Yes	Yes
K	Global pointer	3,5,6,7,9,10	No	No
L	Global pointer	3,5,9	No	No
M	Local pointer	3	No	No
CCFD	Local constant	3	–	–
CCXS3	Local constant	3	–	–
CHAN SELECT	Global variable	2,3	No	No
CONSOLE	Global constant	2,3,5	–	–
PFCN	Local constant	3	–	–
PRINTACW	Local constant	3	–	–
PRINTDATA	Local variable	3	No	No
TYPACW	Global constant	2,3	–	–
USER CORE OFFSET	Global constant	2,3,6	–	–

The major entries required in Noun List 3 are the two character-conversion tables, required because the console operates on Fielddata code, while the remote printers accept a different code, excess three.

The first of these, CCFD, when entered with the numerical value of ICC as an index, returns the numerical value of the appropriate symbol in Fielddata code, while the second, CCXS3, operates in the same way to produce the proper code for the remote printers. The ACW for the printers must contain a count of 135 in bits 18 through 35, and leave room for a starting address in bits 0 through 17.

Noun List 3

```
CCFD[0100] =  075, 056, 053, 055, 042, 041, 050, 074,
              044, 043, 047, 055, 055, 055, 073, 045,
              055, 051, 040, 055, 055, 055, 055, 055,
              055, 072, 055, 060, 061, 062, 063, 064,
              065, 066, 067, 070, 071,  06,  07, 010,
              011, 012, 013, 014, 015, 016, 017, 020,
              021, 022, 023, 024, 025, 026, 027, 030,
              031, 032, 033, 034, 035, 036, 037,  05,
```

```
CCXS3[0100] = 022, 062, 021, 023, 020,  02, 041, 064,
              035, 036, 042, 017, 023, 023, 016, 076,
               01, 061, 075, 063, 023, 023, 037, 023,
              023, 056, 023,  03,  04,  05,  06,  07,
              010, 011, 012, 013, 014, 024, 025, 026,
              027, 030, 031, 032, 033, 034, 044, 045,
              046, 047, 050, 051, 052, 053, 054, 065,
              066, 067, 070, 071, 072, 073, 074,   0,
```

LOCM: 0752400000000,   // Load output channel and monitor.
O1 = 1,
O3 = 3,
O4 = 4,
O110 = 72,
O204 = 132,
PFCN = 011,
PRINTACW = 0207000000   // 135 Print characters.
PRINT DATA;;

    In the PRINT routine, several steps must be taken. First, the absolute address of the user's print image is obtained. This is possible because J was set to the program counter value by the executive return interrupt routine. Next, the physical channel number of the user is obtained. By testing the channel number, it is determined whether the user is the console or a remote device. If the console, then a 72-character line must be converted from ICC to the code used by the console typewriter, and the hardware access control word specified accordingly.

    On the other hand, if the user is a remote device, then a 135-character line must be converted from ICC to the code used by the printer. Following these steps, the routine actually selects the channel and initiates the printing with output monitor interrupt before transferring to select the next ready user. These steps are detailed in Verb List 3, the PRINT routine.

Verb List 3

```
PRINT:
    [J] + USER CORE OFFSET[I] → J,
    CHAN TABLE[I] → CHAN SELECT,
    CHAN SELECT < CONSOLE: P REMOTE.;
        J → M,
        M + O110 → L,
PLOOP2:
    [J] → K,
    CCFD[K] → [J],
    J + O1 → J,
    J < L: PLOOP2.;
        M + TYPACW → PRINT DATA,
        PRINT IO.
```

```
P REMOTE:
    J + O3 → J,
    J → M,
    PFCN → [J],
    J + O1 → J,
    O3 → [J],
    O4 → [J],
    J + O1 → J,
    J + O204 → L,
PLOOP:
    [J] → K,
    CCXS3[K] → [J],
    J + O1 → J,
    J < L: PLOOP.;
    M + PRINTACW → PRINT DATA,
PRINT IO:
    $ LCR, CHAN SELECT;          // Load channel select register
    $ LOCM, PRINT DATA;          // Load output channel and monitor
    NEXT SLICE.
```

At this point it might be useful to return to Verb List J in the compiler, reexamine the code generated by input and output statements, and follow both parts of the process.

Chapter 19

Writing the Interrupt Routines

In this and the following chapters, we will be concerned with seven different hardware interrupts, each of which will transfer control to a specific memory cell when activated. Consequently, we will have to insert into each of these seven cells an instruction further transferring control to the seven routines designed to cope with the requirement posed by the specific interrupt. The details of that process will be deferred until Chapter 22; in the meantime we will merely note that upon activation of any interrupt, the value of the program counter of the interrupted program is stored in the address part of the first word of, and control is transferred to the second word of, the corresponding interrupt routine.

In looking first at the code required to handle the routine *output monitor interrupt* (OUT MON INT), shown in Verb List 4, the following operands will be used.

Operand Table 4

Operand	Class	Used in verb lists	Busy-on-entry	Busy-on-exit
O	Global constant	4,5,6,7,8,9,10	—	—
J	Global pointer	2,3,4,5,6,7,9,10	Yes	Yes
T	Global pointer	4,5	Yes	Yes
BO	Global variable	4,5,8	Yes	No
EXIT 2	Local label	4	No	No
H USER TABLE	Global constant	4,5	—	—
OUT MON INT	Local label	4	Yes	No
READY	Global constant	4,5,9,10	—	—
SAVE J	Global variable	4,5	No	No
SAVE T	Global variable	4,5	No	No
SYSPSR	Global constant	4,5,6,7,9	—	—
USER STATE	Global variable	4,5,6,9,10	No	Yes

Noun List 4 contains several machine language instructions, which serve as operators in crutch code, rather than as operands. Conversely, it must not include the two labels, EXIT 2 and OUT MON INT, even though these labels serve a dual role, and thereby qualify as operands.

Since, as noted in Chapter 16, all interrupts transfer the contents of the user's *processor state register* (PSR) to the first high-speed register, BO, at location zero, it is merely convenient to assign that name to that location. The array H USER TABLE provides for conversion of hardware channel numbers to the corresponding user indices employed by the operating system. Channels which are not serviced by this demonstration system are set at 9, a dummy value. The noun SYSPSR is given that value which, when inserted into the PSR, will place the hardware in open or monitor mode, and cancel the previous guard mode.

Noun List 4

```
AAIJ: 0743400000000,                  // Allow all I/O interrupts and jump.
BO:0,
H USER TABLE[020]  = 9,9,9,9,9,9,9,9,9,9,9,9,1,0,2,9,3,
LPS: 0726400000000,                   // Load PSR.
LPSI: 0726400200000,                  // Load PSR, indirect bit set.
NOP: 0743000000000,                   // No operation.
O = 0,
READY = 1,
SAVE J,
SAVE T,
SCN: 07260000 00000,                  // Store channel number.
SYSPSR = 03 00 00 00 77 000,          // PSR value needed for executive
                                      // Mode. Guard off.
USER STATE[3] ;;                      // Ready, I/O wait, or stop
```

The basic task of the OUT MON INT is merely to notify the system that one of its users has completed printing and should no longer wait for I/O. The process, as detailed in Verb List 4, is as follows. First, the word following the label will receive, in its address field, the address to which return should be made, and control will go directly to the second word. Since the first word therefore represents exit from the interrupt routine, a jump which removes any I/O interrupt lockouts is compiled into this word.

Next, the PSR is set to system mode, which means that the executive set of registers is available to it. Â no operation (NOP) instruction follows it, merely to insure that the requested store is completed before the next instruction is fetched.

The third step provides for the possibility that the operating system itself, rather than a user program, was interrupted by saving two of its important registers, *T* and *J*.

By storing the channel number in *J* and consulting the hardware channel number assignment table, it obtains the actual user index, and accomplishes the objective of resetting that user's state to ready. At this point it transfers the instruction following the entry point to the exit, restores its own registers, restores the user's value to the PSR, waits for that to be completed, and returns to the program it was previously executing.

Verb List 4

```
OUT MON INT:
    $ AAIJ, 0;
    $ LPSI, SYSPSR;
    $ NOP, 0;
    T → SAVE T,
    J → SAVE J,
    $ SCN, J;
    H USER TABLE[J] → J,
    READY → USER STATE[J],
    OUT MON INT → Exit 2,
    SAVE J → J,
    SAVE T → T,
    $ LPS, BO;
    $ NOP, O;
EXIT 2:
    $ AAIJ, O;;
```

In this routine, did you notice that your Pilot compiler can move any instruction from one labeled point to another? This capability will be exploited more fully in initializing the system. Clearly, in Verb List 4, the crutch-coded instruction following the label EXIT 2 will be overlaid by the first instruction in the routine, after the address field of that instruction has received its return address. Consequently, the presence of the final AAIJ (allow all interrupts and jump) instruction is redundant, serving only to increase the clarity.

The task of the input monitor interrupt routine, to be shown in Verb List 5, is basically, the same as the previous routine, in that it must return a user to ready status, but in addition it takes over the function of converting from the input code of either the console typewriter or any of the remote devices to internal compiler code (ICC). Prior to the implementation of the operating system, this conversion was done within the compiler.

The operands which will be used by IN MON INT are given in Operand Table 5.

The basic entries in Noun List 5, which follows, are the arrays used for the conversion of characters from either the console typewriter or the remote card readers into ICC. In addition, the control register location of an input access control word (ACW), octal 40, is assigned to LOC IACW.

Operand Table 5

Operand	Class	Used in verb lists	Busy-on-entry	Busy-on-exit
O	Global constant	4,5,6,7,8,9,10	—	—
O1	Global constant	3,5,6,7,9,10	—	—
O110	Global constant	3,5	—	—
O120	Local constant	5	—	—
J	Global pointer	2,3,4,5,6,7,9,10	Yes	Yes
K	Global pointer	3,5,6,7,9,10	Yes	Yes
L	Global pointer	3,5,9	Yes	Yes
T	Global pointer	4,5	Yes	Yes
BO	Global variable	4,5,8	Yes	No
CONSOLE	Global constant	2,3,5	—	—
EXIT 1	Local label	5,	No	No
FDCC	Local constant	5	—	—
H USER TABLE	Global constant	4,5	—	—
IN MON INT	Local label	5	Yes	No
LOC IACW	Local constant	5	—	—
READY	Global constant	4,5,9,10	—	—
SAVE J	Global variable	4,5	No	No
SAVE K	Local variable	5	No	No
SAVE L	Local variable	5	No	No
SAVE T	Global variable	4,5	No	No
SYSPSR	Global constant	4,5,6,7,9	—	—
USER STATE	Global variable	4,5,6,9,10	No	Yes
XS3CC	Local constant	5	—	—

Noun List 5

```
FDCC[0100]  = 077, 077, 077, 077, 077, 077, 045, 046,
              047, 050, 051, 052, 053, 054, 055, 056,
              057, 060, 061, 062, 063, 064, 065, 066,
              067, 070, 071, 072, 073, 074, 075, 076,
              022,  05,  04, 011, 044, 017, 077, 047,
              06, 021, 077,  02, 077,  03,  01, 077,
              033, 034, 035, 036, 037, 040, 041, 042,
              043, 044, 031, 016,  07,   0, 077, 077,
LOC IACW = 040,                        // Address of first input ACW
                                       // for recovery of absolute
                                       // image address.

O120 = 80,
SAVE K,
SAVE L,
XS3CC[0100] = 077, 020,  05, 033, 034, 035, 036, 037,
              040, 041, 042, 043, 044, 012, 016, 013,
              04, 023,   0, 024, 045, 046, 047, 050,
              051, 052, 053, 054, 055, 010, 011, 026,
              027,  06, 012, 013, 056, 057, 060, 061,
              062, 063, 064, 065, 066, 030, 031, 025,
              03, 021,  01,  02,  07, 067, 070, 071,
              072, 073, 074, 075, 076, 022, 017, 030;;
```

The process followed in the input monitor interrupt (IN MON INT) routine is the same as the previous one only to the point at which the USER STATE is reset to READY. Then the routine obtains the input ACW address by adding the channel number to the base address, IACW. This word contains the absolute address of the last character. Since the console transmits 72 characters, and the remote devices send 80, the address of the first character can be found by subtraction after the nature of the sender is determined. In either case, table conversion is completed before resuming the same pattern studied in Verb List 4.

Verb List 5

```
IN MON INT:
    $ AAIJ, O;
    $ LPSI, SYSPSR;
    $ NOP, O;
    T → SAVE T,
    J → SAVE J,
    K → SAVE K,
    L → SAVE L,
    $ SCN, J;                        // Channel Nr → J
    H USER TABLE [J] → K,
    READY → USER STATE[K],
    LOC IACW + J → K,
    J < CONSOLE: CONV REMOTE.;
        [K] → L,
        L - 0110 → K,
RLOOP 2:        .
        [K] → J,
        FDCC[J] → [K],
        K + O1 → K,
        K < L: RLOOP 2.;
    BACK.
CONV REMOTE:
    [K] → L,
    L - 0120 → K,
RLOOP:
    [K] → J,
    XS3CC[J] → [K],
    K + O1 → K,
    K < L: RLOOP.;
BACK:
    IN MON INT → EXIT 1,
    SAVE J → J,
    SAVE K → K,
    SAVE L → L,
    SAVE T → T,
    $ LPS, BO;
    $ NOP, O;
EXIT 1:
    $ AAIJ, O;
```

Chapter 20

The Executive Return

The executive return interrupt is generated internally, whenever the non-privileged instruction ER is executed in any program. The basic function of the code which must be executed whenever the operating system is thus called directly by a user program consists of filing the user's program counter and process state register (PSR), initiating the indicated input or output, setting the user in a wait state, and returning, either directly or through READ or PRINT, to select the next user. The details of this process are given in Verb List 6, which employs the operands in Operand Table 6.

Operand Table 6

Operand	Class	Used in verb lists	Busy-on-entry	Busy-on-exit
O	Global constant	4,5,6,7,8,9,10	—	—
O1	Global constant	3,5,6,7,9,10	—	—
030000	Local constant	6	—	—
I	Global pointer	2,3,6,7,9,10	Yes	Yes
J	Global pointer	2,3,4,5,6,7,9,10	No	No
K	Global pointer	3,5,6,7,9,10	No	No
S	Local pointer	6	No	No
BA	Global variable	6,7,10	Yes	Yes
BASE LIM	Local constant	6	—	—
ER	Local label	6	Yes	No
ERPRINT	Local constant	6	—	—
ERREAD	Local constant	6	—	—
IO WAIT	Local constant	6	—	—
MAX BA	Global constant	6,7,10	—	—
NR USERS	Global constant	6,7,9,10	—	—
PREG	Local variable	6	No	Yes
PSR	Global variable	6,10	No	Yes
STOP	Local constant	6	—	—
SYSPSR	Global constant	4,5,6,7,9	—	—
USER CORE OFFSET	Global constant	2,3,6,	—	—
USER STATE	Global variable	4,5,6,9,10	No	Yes

Noun List 6 contains those constants and variables not previously used. The array BA is defined to provide space for storing the 14 working registers of an interrupted program. The array PSR provides user-state values which, when loaded into the PSR of the computer will place it in guard mode, and the low-order nine bits of which specify the address, in octal thousands, from which the user's data area will float.

Noun List 6

BA[56],   // Control register storage
BASE LIMIT = 010000,
ER PRINT = 0724400000002,   // See Verb List J.
ER READ = 0724400000001,   // See Verb List J.
MAX BA = 14,
NR USERS = 2,
030000 = 030000
PREG[2] = 03020, 03020,   // Initially set to start of
                                             // reentrant control card processor

PSR[2] = 04030007110, 04030007120,
STOP = 3;;   // Flag for USER STATE

The details of the executive return procedure are shown in Verb List 6, where the first word is used to receive the value of the user's program counter upon interrupt. The first-executed instruction will put the system in executive mode by loading the PSR with the appropriate system value. After a NOP (no operation) instruction to allow time for the previous instruction to be completed, the stored value of the user's program counter is picked up and examined to see whether it pointed to the user's data area or to his instruction area. The relative value is then made absolute, and stored in the appropriate word of the program counter array, PREG. The user's value of the PSR will have been temporarily stored in cell zero by the interrupt, and it is returned to the file, or PSR array.

Next, the contents of the 14 user registers are stored in the array BA, the user's state is reduced to wait for I/O, and his request is examined. This is done by looking at the word in the user's program which triggered the interrupt, which can be found by looking one word ahead of the absolute address given by his program counter.

The program counter itself is then passed, in *J*, to either READ or PRINT, whichever is called, or the user is terminated by reducing his USER STATE to STOP.

Verb List 6

ER:
    $ O, 0;
    $ LPSI, SYSPSR;
    $ NOP, 0;
    ER → S,
    S < BASE LIM: INSTR CASE.;

DATA CASE:
    S + USER CORE OFFSET[I] → S,
    READY 1.

INSTR CASE:
    S + 030000 → S,

READY 1:
    S + O1 → PREG[I],
    OO → J,
    [J] → PSR[I],
    I → K,

UNLOAD:
    [J] → BA[K],
    K + NR USERS → K,
    J + O1 → J,
    J < MAX BA: UNLOAD.;
    IO WAIT → USER STATE[I],
    S → J,
    J − OI → S,
    [S] = ERREAD: READ.;
    [S] = ER PRINT: PRINT.;
        STOP → USER STATE[I],
        NEXT SLICE.

Chapter 21

Clock Interrupts

The internal clock, located at cell 64, counts down at the rate of 5000 bits per second, and produces an interrupt when it reaches zero. When a user's time slice is exhausted, it is only necessary to file his instruction counter, save his working registers, leave his user state as it was, and continue with the next user. The details of the process, which first returns the processor state register (PSR) to the operating system mode, are given in Verb List 7, which employs the operands listed in Operand Table 7.

Operand Table 7

Operand	Class	Used in verb lists	Busy-on-entry	Busy-on-exit
O	Global constant	4,5,6,7,8,9,10	—	—
O1	Global constant	3,5,6,7,9,10	—	—
I	Global pointer	2,3,6,7,9,10	Yes	Yes
J	Global pointer	2,3,4,5,6,7,9,10	No	No
K	Global pointer	3,5,6,7,9,10	No	No
BA	Global variable	6,7,10	No	Yes
CLOCK	Local label	7	Yes	No
MAX BA	Global constant	6,7,10	—	—
NR USERS	Global constant	6,7,9,10	—	—
PREG	Global variable	6,7,10	No	Yes
SYSPSR	Global constant	4,5,6,7,9,	—	—

Since all of the nouns used in Verb List 7 have appeared in earlier declaration statements, Noun List 7 is empty. The real-time clock interrupt routine is the one shown in Verb List 7.

Verb List 7

```
CLOCK:
    $ 0, 0;
    $ LPSI, SYSPSR;
    $ NOP, 0;
```

```
CLOCK → PREG[I],
I → K,
O → J,
UNLOD 2:
    [J] → BA[K],
    K + NR USERS → K,
    J + O1 → J,
    J < MAX BA: UNLOD 2.;
        NEXT SLICE.
```

In addition to the real-time clock, the 1108 has a day clock which must be disarmed, since it is not used by the simple operating system, but will generate interrupts nevertheless. The four instructions required to provide the bypass for this clock are given in Verb List 8, which uses only the three operands listed.

Operand Table 8

Operand	Class	Used in verb lists	Busy-on-entry	Busy-on-exit
O	Global constant	4,5,6,7,8,9,10	—	—
BO	Global variable	4,5,8	Yes	No
EXIT CK	Local label	8	No	No

Again, the routine does not use any previously undeclared constants or variables, hence Noun List 8 is also empty.

The label CLOCKS in Verb List 8 should not be confused with the singular form used in the previous routine. Now the result of this interrupt will cause the address to which return is desired to be placed in the address field of the instruction immediately following the label CLOCKS, and transfer control to the next instruction, from which a direct jump to the start of the routine will produce a return of the PSR to the user value. From there, control will fall through to the instruction which returns control to the interrupted user.

Verb List 8

```
EXIT CK:
    $ LPS, BO;
    $ NOP, O;
CLOCKS:
    $ AAIJ, O;
    $ JI, EXIT CK;
```

Since this routine serves the function of short-circuiting an interrupt it can, and will, be used temporarily to bypass other interrupts while the operating system is being initialized.

Chapter 22

Setting Up the System

Before the time-slicing system described in the previous sections can be put into execution, a number of initialization functions must be completed. The first of these requires that the mini-operating system (mini-OS) being described be slid into the computer and usurp the function of its previous operating system.

Since the mini-OS must be compiled by a version of the Pilot compiler running under the previous OS, the actual execution of the new OS must be delayed until all listings from that compilation have been completed. This is accomplished by having the new OS hold until key 1 on the console is set by the operator. Since control will be transferred to the location specified by PRO-GRAM START as soon as the new system has been compiled, the first statement in the system must be a jump to the initialization routine.

As soon as the operator signals that the listings are complete, by depressing the console key, the new system must inhibit all interrupts, remove the memory lockout limits, so that it will be able to write instructions into the interrupt cells, set the Processor State Register (PSR) in the new system's mode, duplicate copies of the basic data area, set all users to ready, initialize the interrupt cells, clear all I/O channels, set the user index, I, to zero and jump to the user's selection routine.

In the process of inserting the required jump instructions in the interrupt cells, a problem arises. Since the addresses which are required will depend upon compilation, these addresses are unavailable prior to compilation. This problem is solved by actually compiling the required instructions, complete with their required transfer addresses, at some other location. Then, by means of their labels, these compiled instructions are inserted into the proper interrupt cells. Note, therefore, that the last seven labels in this verb list do not represent entry points to which control is ever transferred, but that this fact does not indicate that they could be eliminated.

The initialization routine, called COLD START, makes use of the operands given in Operand Table 9.

In addition to a number of machine language instructions not previously declared, Noun List 9 must contain the absolute low-core addresses of seven of the interrupt locations. These are the locations to which control is automatically transferred when its specific interrupt occurs.

Operand Table 9

Operand	Class	Used in verb lists	Busy-on-entry	Busy-on-exit
O	Global constant	4,5,6,7,8,9,10	—	—
O1	Global constant	3,5,6,7,9,10	—	—
O10000	Local constant	10	—	—
O120000	Local constant	10	—	—
O130000	Local constant	10	—	—
I	Global pointer	2,3,6,7,9,10	No	Yes
J	Global pointer	2,3,4,5,6,7,9,10	No	No
K	Global pointer	3,5,6,7,9,10	No	No
L	Global pointer	3,5,9	No	No
CHAN	Local variable	9	No	No
DCIC	Global label	9,10	Yes	Yes
ERIC	Local label	9	Yes	No
IIIC	Local label	9	Yes	No
IMIC	Local label	9	Yes	No
LOC DCIC	Local constant	9	—	—
LOC ERIC	Local constant	9	—	—
LOC IIIC	Local constant	9	—	—
LOC IMIC	Local constant	9	—	—
LOC MLIC	Local constant	9	—	—
LOC OMIC	Local constant	9	—	—
LOC RCIC	Global constant	9,10	—	—
MLIC	Local label	9	Yes	No
NR CHANS	Local constant	9	—	—
NR USERS	Global constant	6,7,9,10	—	—
OMIC	Local label	9	Yes	No
RCIC	Global label	9,10	Yes	Yes
READY	Global constant	4,5,9,10	—	—
SLSLSL	Local constant	9	—	—
SYSPSR	Global constant	4,5,6,7,9	—	—
USER STATE	Global variable	4,5,6,9,10	No	Yes

Noun List 9

CHAN,
DIC: 0751400000000,   // Disconnect input channel
                                    // specified by channel select
                                    // register.
DOC: 0753400000000,   // Same as DIC, but output.
HJ: 0742400000000,   // Halt then jump.
JI: 0742000200000,   // Jump indirect.

JK1: 0742020000000,   // Jump if key 1 set.
LSL: 0727000000000,   // Load storage limits register.
LOC IMIC = 0220,   // Location of the input monitor
                                           // interrupt cell.
LOC OMIC = 0221,   // Output monitor interrupt
                                           // cell location.
LOC RCIC = 0231,   // Real-time clock interrupt
                                           // cell location.
LOC IIIC = 0241,   // Illegal instruction interrupt
                                           // cell location.
LOC ERIC = 0242,   // Executive return interrupt
                                           // cell location (return for
                                           // user to system).
LOC MLIC = 0243,   // Memory lockout error interrupt
                                           // cell location.
LOC DCIC = 0217,   // Day clock interrupt cell location.
NR CHANS = 16,
O10: 01000000,
// Constants for system layout:
O10000 = 010000,
O120000 = 0120000,
O130000 = 0130000,
PAIJ: 0725400000000,   // Permit all I/O interrupts
                                           // and jump.
SLJI: 0720400200000,   // Store location and jump
                                           // indirect.
SYSLSL = 0177000177000;;   // Value for the storage limit
                                           // register which unlocks core.

In addition to the tasks noted earlier, the routine COLD START duplicates a 10000-octal word data area for each user, starting at address 0120000. Note that the individual value of the PSRs assigned to each user in Noun List 6 contains a data-base address with which Verb List 9 must conform.

Verb List 9

```
COLD START: PAUSE.
PAUSE:
    $JK1, INHIBIT INTERRUPTS;
    PAUSE.

INHIBIT INTERRUPTS:
    $PAIJ, OPEN MEMORY;

OPEN MEMORY:
    $LSL, SYSLSL;
    $LPS, SYSPSR;
    $NOP, O;
    O1 → L,

MOVE DATA AREA:
    0120000 → J,
```

```
    O130000 → K,
SET MOVE:
    O → I,
MOVE MORE:
    [J] → [K],
    K + O1 → K,
    J + O1 → J,
    I + O1 → I,
    I < O10000: MOVE MORE.;
        O120000 → J,
        L + O1 → L,
        L < NR USERS: SET MOVE.;
            O → J,
SET ALL USERS:
    READY → USER STATE[J],
    J + O1 → J,
    J < NR USERS: SET ALL USERS.;
LOAD INTERRUPT CELLS:
    LOC DCIC → I,
    DCIC → [I],
    LOC ERIC → I,
    ERIC → [I],
    LOC IMIC → I,
    IMIC → [I],
    LOC OMIC → I,
    OMIC → [I],
    LOC RCIC → I,
    DCIC → [I],
    LOC IIIC → I,
    IIIC → [I],
    LOC MLIC → I,
    MLIC → [I],
    O → CHAN,
CLEAR CHANNELS:
    $ LCR, CHAN;
    $ DIC, 0;
    $ DOC, 0;
    CHAN + O1 → CHAN,
    CHAN < NR CHANS: CLEAR CHANNELS.;
        O → I,
        NEXT SLICE.
//  Following seven statements compiled here for use elsewhere.
    ERIC: $SLJI, ER;
    IMIC: $SLJI, OUT MON INT;
    RCIC: $SLJI, CLOCK;
    IIIC: $SLJI, IIIC2:
//  IIC2 merely provides space for an illegal instruction's address.
    IIIC2: $O, 0;
    MLIC: $HJ, 0;
    DCIC: $SLJI, CLOCKS;
```

In the preceding routine, did you notice that the day-clock interrupt instruction was inserted both in its proper place, and in the interrupt cell reserved for the real-time clock? As a consequence, since the day-clock instructions actually ignore that interrupt, even the real-time clock will not interrupt the operating system until this cell is changed, as it will be in the routine to which it transfers, NEXT SLICE.

Chapter 23

A Simple Scheduler

The last routine required for the operating system, called NEXT SLICE, is actually a very simple scheduler. It must provide for: (1) selecting the next user; (2) setting his program counter; (3) restoring his working registers; (4) authorizing a unit of time; (5) setting his allocated memory limits; (6) putting the system in user mode; and (7) transferring control to the proper instruction in the user program. The operands which it uses are given in Operand Table 10.

Operand Table 10

Operand	Class	Used in verb lists	Busy-on-entry	Busy-on-exit
O	Global constant	4,5,6,7,8,9,10	—	—
O1	Global constant	3,5,6,7,9,10	—	—
I	Global pointer	2,3,6,7,9,10	Yes	Yes
J	Global pointer	2,3,4,5,6,7,9,10	No	No
K	Global pointer	3,5,6,7,9,10	No	No
BA	Global variable	6,7,10	Yes	No
DCIC	Global label	9,10	Yes	No
LOC CLOCK	Local constant	10	—	—
LOC RCIC	Global constant	9,10	—	—
MAX BA	Global constant	6,7,10	—	—
MAX SLICE	Local constant	10	—	—
NR USERS	Global constant	6,7,9,10	—	—
PREG	Global variable	6,7,10	Yes	No
PSR	Global constant	6,10	—	—
RCIC	Global label	9,10	Yes	No
READY	Global constant	4,5,9,10	—	—
SAVE PSR	Local variable	10	No	No
USER INDEX	Local variable	10	No	Yes
USER STATE	Global variable	4,5,6,9,10	Yes	Yes

Those constants, variables and machine instructions which have not heretofore been declared are entered in Noun List 10.

Noun List 10

AACI: 0756000000000,   // Allow all channel interrupts
                                                  // and jump.
LOC CLOCK = 0100,   // Holds the real-time clock
                                                  // Count
MAX SLICE = 4999,   // One second of time
USER INDEX; ;

The last routine required by the operating system is given in Verb List 10.

Verb List 10

```
NEXT SLICE:
    LOC RCIC → J,
    DCIC → [J],
    $ AACI, ALLOW IO INT;

ALLOW IO INT:
    $ AAIJ, CYCLE;

CYCLE:
    I + O1 → I,
    I < NR USERS: TEST READY. ;
    O → I,

TEST READY:
    USER STATE[I] = READY: START USER. ;
        CYCLE.

START USER:
    OO → J,
    I → USER INDEX,
    I → K,

LOAD:
    BA[K] → J,
    K + NR USERS → K,
    J + O1 → J,
    J < MAX BA: LOAD. ;
        LOC CLOCK → K,
        MAX SLICE → [K],
        LOC RCIC → K,
        RCIC → [K],
        PSR[K] → SAVE PSR,
        PREG[I] → J,
        $ LPS, SAVE PSR;
        [J].
```

Once the operating system enters this routine, it will not leave until it finds a user program which is in the READY state. Until it does so, it will ignore all clock interrupts. I/O interrupts, however, are not inhibited. Therefore, user states may become READY while this routine is cycling.

At this point all of the routines required for the implementation of both the compiler and the time-slicing operating system have been examined in complete detail. Once they have been implemented and tested on another computer, they are in condition for rapid improvement and extension.

Epilogue

Suggested Extensions

Many possible extensions to the basic compiler can be made quite easily, while others require more time and effort. Extensions to the operating system, on the other hand, invariably involve large amounts of dedicated computer time, which is seldom available. Consequently, this final chapter will merely mention features which have been added to the basic compiler.

Furthermore, no attempt will be made to indicate possible methods of implementation. The comparative difficulty of implementation, on the other hand, will be given rather roughly on a scale of 0 to 20, where 50 might represent the effort previously expended.

Extension 1: Extended relationals in comparison. Difficulty = 0.5. Write and insert generators for the relationals $>$, $\geqslant$, $\neq$, and $\leqslant$ in the comparison statement.

Extension 2: Multiple assignments. Difficulty = 0.5. Provide for assignment statements of the form: A→B→C→D,

Extension 3: Left-to-right precedence. Difficulty = 0.5. Without providing for higher precedence of multiplication and division over addition and subtraction, provide for compiling statements of the form:

$$A \times B / C + D - E \rightarrow F,.$$

This feature can be implemented without any new generators by providing the appropriate entries in the CO–NO table.

Extension 4: Extend comparisons to expressions. Difficulty = 0.5. Permit a comparison statement to be written with any expression on the left of the relational operator, as:

$$A \times B + C < D:$$

or

$$A \times B + C \rightarrow D = E:$$

Note that providing the same capability on the right of the relational is quite feasible, but has a difficulty factor of about 5.0.

Extension 5: Boolean operators. Difficulty = 1.5. Provide generators to allow statements of the form:

$$A \wedge B \to C,$$
and
$$E \vee F \to G,$$

Extension 6: Negative numbers. Difficulty = 1.5. Provide for unary minus, to remove this restriction from the basic compiler.

Extension 7: Alpha-numeric literals. Difficulty = 2.0. Provide for the use of numeric literals in the verb list.

Extension 8: Exchange operator. Difficulty = 2.0. Provide an exchange statement. In addition to a generator, this extension requires the selection of two operators whose use in a CO–NO pair was previously illegal, such as > followed by <, to give a statement of the form:

$$A[I] \times A[J],.$$

This statement type was first used in the Jovial compilers, and proved most useful.

Extension 9: Shift operation. Difficulty = 2.5. Provide for right or left shifts of operands by any number of bits. For consistency of design, this has often been implemented by statements of the form:

$$A \times 2 \uparrow B \to C,$$
and
$$A / 2 \uparrow B \to C,$$

where the exponent is tested first. If it is a 2, then shifting is generated, but if it is not a 2, then it is illegal, until extension 10 has been implemented.

Extension 10: Exponentiation. Difficulty = 2.5. Provide an exponentiation routine, and generate a call upon it when the symbol $\uparrow$ is encountered. Avoid the call when the exponent is a 2.

Extension 11: Location operator. Difficulty = 3.0. Provide the ability to reference the location of an operand. This is most easily done in the noun list, by providing for declarations of the form:

$$X,$$
$$Y = \{X\},$$

and providing that the variable Y be given as its initial value, the address of X. A more convenient form can implemented in verb lists, by noting that the left brace occurs in the CO–NO table only after a colon. It is therefore possible to implement a statement such as:

$$10 + \{X\} \to Z,.$$

Extension 12: Bit handling. Difficulty = 5.0. Again, this extension can be implemented either in the noun list or in the verb list, but the latter seems to provide less chance for error on the part of the user. A form which fits the design, and yet leaves the use of parentheses available for later use in parenthetical grouping of arithmetic expressions, is:

$$A(0{\rightarrow}5) + B[J](6{\rightarrow}7) \rightarrow A(0{\rightarrow}6),.$$

A point to note is that the specification of the bits involved should follow, rather than preceed, the index for an array.

Extension 13: Double subscripting. Difficulty = 10. While systems languages have little need for this feature, general-purpose languages require it, and its implementation is most interesting.

Extension 14: Loops. Difficulty = 10. Since the fundamental power of the digital computer lies in its use in iteration, any language without a loop statement might be ruled inadequate. This feature may be specified in many ways, one of which is of the form:

$$I = A(B)C \left\{ \qquad\qquad \right\},$$

where the index, I, is given the initial value A, the increment is B, and its final value is C. The material to be repeated is that enclosed between the braces.

Extension 15: Nested loops. Difficulty = 10 + 5 = 15. Using the same form adopted in extension 14, provide, by means of push-down stacks in the compiler, for nesting of loops to a depth of at least eight. Note that while loops may be nested, they may not be overlapped.

Extension 16: Relocation. Difficulty = 10. If relocatable code was not generated originally, this capability may be added as an extension.

Extension 17: Open comparisons. Difficulty = 10. The basic comparison statement may readily be extended to one of the form:

$$A = B: S_1 ; S_2 ; S_3$$

Where S_1 represents the statements to be executed if the condition is true, S_2 represents the statements to be executed if the condition is false, and S_3 represents the statements to be executed after either S_1 or S_2 statements have been executed.

Extension 18: Nested comparisons. Difficulty = 10+2=12. Provide for the ability to include any conditional statement as one of the statements making up either S_1 or S_2 in extension 17. This is a most interesting extension, and can actually provide for the generation of extremely efficient code.

Extension 19: Precedence expressions. Difficulty = 15. Provide for the proper coding of arithmetic expressions of any length and complexity according to operator precedence, and allowing for the use of parenthesis. This will require that, once an arithmetic expression is encountered, the current operator (CO) be assigned to a push-down stack.

Extension 20: Register optimization. Difficulty = 20. For any machine with multiple accumulators, the proper use of these registers will result in a dramatic improvement in efficiency, hence this extension can be most rewarding.

Extension 21: Incorporating extensions into compiler source. Each extension which has been added to the source language which the compiler will handle represents also a feature which could have been used to advantage, had it existed, at the time the first version of the compiler was written in source language. By rewriting the source in the higher-level language provided by the extensions, two advantages will be found. First, the number of source statements of the compiler will be reduced, and second, the compile speed will be increased.

Index